THE MUSIC OF INDIA

The classical music of the India-Pakistan-Bangladesh subcontinent is one of the few ancient art forms still widely practised today. In recent years it has been much appreciated all over the world. This book, written by Indian writers, serves to deepen that appreciation to understanding. It covers the philosophy and history of Indian music clearly and concisely and relates its growth and development to social, cultural, religious and political factors. India's musical contacts with the East and the West are also discussed and their value assessed.

The technical chapters explain the *raga* and *tala* systems, the numerous instruments from north and south are described in detail with the help of excellent line drawings by Eilean Pearcey, and the glossary of terms illumines the subject in an interesting way. Short biographies of established musicians, composers and musicologists place on record their various achievements. Apart from a selective bibliography and discography for the reader's guidance there is also a list of useful addresses.

The Music of India will prove invaluable to the student and specialist who requires a ready handbook on the subject. For the general reader it contains a mine of information on the musical life of an entire subcontinent.

Ravi Shankar, in his Foreword, recommends this book to all who wish to be introduced to India's music, her culture and her peoples.

This is a work of scholarship; lively, at times even witty and *never* dull.

Reginald Massey, poet, writer and critic has studied Indian music and dance for many years and has written on these subjects for *The Times, The Guardian, The Musical Times, Music and Musicians, The Illustrated Weekly of India* and other journals. He has written the Indian music entry for *Everyman's Encyclopaedia* and the Asian dance section for *The Encyclopaedia of Dance and Ballet.* He is a *Dancing Times* critic and *The Dances of India* which he and his wife have co-authored, is a recognized work in the literature of dance.

He writes film and television scripts.

A Fellow of the Royal Society of Arts, he is listed in many international writers' directories and biographical dictionaries.

Jamila Massey, actress and writer, was educated at London University's King's College. She writes children's stories. Deeply interested and involved in music, she has introduced several Indian musicians and dancers to audiences in the West. She and her husband have collaborated on a novel, *The Immigrants,* which is set in India, Pakistan and the United Kingdom.

Reginald and Jamila Massey constitute a for partnership.

for
Marcus Iqbal Ravi
each to each

THE MUSIC OF
INDIA

by Reginald & Jamila Massey
foreword by Ravi Shankar

KAHN & AVERILL
LONDON

This revised edition first published in 1993 by
Kahn and Averill
9 Harrington Road, London SW7 3ES

British Library Cataloguing in Publication Data

A catalogue record for this book is available from the British Library

ISBN-1-871082-50-1

Printed in Great Britain by
Halstan & Co Ltd., Amersham, Bucks.

Contents

Acknowledgements

The authors wish to acknowledge the help given by the following persons and organizations in the preparation of this book:
Ayub Aulia; Sarah Chohan; Greenwich Borough Libraries; India Office Library, London; Morris Kahn; Mathoor Krishnamurti of the Bharatiya Vidya Bhavan, London; Nala Najan; Eilean Pearcey; Raji; Ravi Shankar; Robert Skelton of the Victoria & Albert Museum; Sama Swaminathan; Maureen Travis of the India House Library, London; Betty Tyers of the Victoria & Albert Museum; Ajay K. Varma.

List of Illustrations

Foreword

by Ravi Shankar

Music, the greatest art of my country, has the unique quality of appealing directly to the hearts and minds of men. Indian music, especially, has this quality in abundance for it is rooted in Nature itself. Nevertheless, a basic knowledge of the history and principles of the art can only help towards a greater appreciation and understanding.

During recent years a number of books on Indian music have appeared in various parts of the world and some of them have been admirable contributions to musical literature. Others, however, have caused more confusion than clarification. It is to clear this confusion that Reginald and Jamila Massey have written this book. Their work, lucidly expounded, sets Indian music in the wider context of India's culture and historical progress and provides an excellent foundation course.

It is, therefore, with pleasure that I recommend this book to all who wish to be introduced to India's music, her culture and her peoples.

Ravi Shankar

1 The Vedic Heritage

Man is a creative animal and the noblest monument to the spirit of Man is the art and science of music. From time immemorial Man has made music to add a further dimension to his expression of the magical or the mystical, the emotional or the martial. Because he is also able to analyse, interpret and distinguish, Man found some sounds in Nature pleasing and others not. He found meanings in the songs of birds and discovered rhythm in the movements of the heavenly bodies.

Music exists in all societies. It functions in the sphere of religion and through the whole of Man's experience to the area of pure entertainment. It has, therefore, many forms — some very new, or at least seemingly so, and others of great antiquity.

Indian music, in its classical forms, is one of the most ancient types still surviving. It has, of course, altered but its basic elements would appear to be much as they were over two thousand years ago.

The earliest cities discovered on the subcontinent of India were Mohenjo Daro and Harappa in the Indus valley. This civilization, highly organized and developed, was coeval with that of the Nile valley. From the excavations carried out under Sir Mortimer Wheeler there is evidence that the seven-holed flute and various types of stringed instruments and drums were in use in these two cities. Indeed, these musical instruments must have been used and perfected hundreds of years before they came into the hands of the expert musicians and dancing girls of Mohenjo Daro and Harappa.

Around 2000 B.C., the Aryans came to the subcontinent through the passes in the North-West and with their coming

India entered the Vedic period of her history. Many theories about the coming of the Aryans to India have been expounded and demolished over the years. The most plausible at the moment seems to be the one put forward by Nirad Chaudhuri; namely, that after leaving the region between the Danube and the Volga some Aryan tribes settled in Mesopotamia, then pushed into Iran and, later, found their way into northern India which came to be called Aryavarta, the land of the Aryans.

The Aryans were a fair-skinned people whereas the indigenous inhabitants of India were dark. After they had subjugated the country, the Aryans organized the caste system so as to maintain their supremacy. They introduced their own culture and religion and, in their turn, adapted some local customs and even gods. This was made easier by the fact that they settled down with the intention of coexisting with the original inhabitants of their new homeland.

The caste system allowed for many gradations in the social scale and it was worked out in such great detail and so interlocked with religion and economic conditions, that it operated without creating tensions. It brought about a division of labour in a way which eliminated the need for slavery, and consequently this institution never existed in ancient India. The Brahmins were the priests and intellectuals, the Kshatriyas the warriors, the Vaishyas the merchants, and the Shudras the manual workers. The sub-castes related to specific professions; for example, among the Brahmins there was a sub-caste of physicians, the Kshatriyas had a sub-caste of archers, Vaishyas had a sub-caste of money-lenders, and the Shudras had a sub-caste of cobblers. In the arts there were sub-castes which specialized in music, in painting and in dancing. All of these functioned as hereditary guilds. In the area of the arts this ensured that certain forms, techniques and styles were passed on from father to son in an unbroken tradition. In its later years, the caste system became a harsh instrument of man's inhumanity to man and it has now been abolished by law. There can be little doubt, however, that it is thanks to this system that India's music and dance have been handed down over hundreds of years with all the respect and love that a great heritage richly deserves.

The Aryan Brahmins produced great thinkers and scholars

yet, strangely, they never wrote any histories; instead all subjects, including history, were presented in mythological form and given religious sanction by being associated with the gods.

Religious sanction always makes ideas much more invulnerable, and so legends grew around the history of the Aryans, beginning with the *Rig-Veda* and culminating in the two epics of the *Ramayana* and the *Mahabharata*. All learning was embodied in books called *shastras*. Each *shastra* covers its subject in detail and represents, obviously, not the inspiration of a single man, but the accumulation of a tradition codified in one volume. In the same way, the works of Homer could not have been produced out of the darkness of a barbaric society, but represent the pinnacle of a long-standing culture.

Brahmin *gurus* considered that the highest knowledge was too valuable, perhaps even dangerous, to be lightly bestowed upon all men and were careful to pass it on only to those who were worthy of it and were capable of using it with discrimination. To make sure that it did not fall into the wrong hands it was expressed in symbolic terms and complicated riddle-like verses or *mantras* which had to be interpreted like the Greek oracles and the books by mediaeval alchemists.

The sacred scriptures consisted of the four main Vedas — the *Rig-Veda*, the *Yajur-Veda*, the *Sam-Veda* and the *Atharva-Veda*, and several minor ones. These, together with the two epics and the various *Puranas* or stories concerning the gods, had a close connection with music for the verses were chanted in set musical patterns. This early form of vocal music was known as *Sāmagān* from *sāma* meaning 'melody' and *gān* meaning 'to sing verses'. There were only three tonal accents — *udātta, anudātta* and *svarita* — which were later named *swaras*, musical notes. Eventually, a total of seven *swaras* was identified and came into use. However, even today the *Vedas* can be heard chanted to the three accented musical pattern.

As the *Vedas* underwent modifications and additions so also did *Sāmagān*. The pre-Aryan music also developed at the same time and there was considerable cross-fertilization with the result that a form called *Jātigān* emerged. This depended on the use of *jatis* or sequences of notes and was the precursor of what was later to become the *raga* system.

The Brahmins now divided music into two categories: *Mārga Sangeet* — that which was 'pleasing to the gods' and which was sacred music — and *Desi Sangeet* — that which was 'pleasing to humans' and which was secular or profane music. Both used the seven *swaras* but in *Mārga Sangeet* the melodic patterns were clearly defined as falling into seven classes: *ārcik* used one note, *gāthik* two, *sāmik* three, *swarāntar* four, *odava* five, *sādava* six, and *sampūrna* seven. It is clear, therefore, that sacred music, the idiom in which the religious texts were sung in the temples, received more serious attention.

In south India there are still families of Brahmins who devote their whole lives to the exact and proper chanting of the holy books; sometimes a priest will concentrate on one particular epic exclusively simply in order to attain perfection in his rendering of it. One such was the late Panchpakesa Bhagvatar who could keep his audience enthralled for hours at a time. His chanting of the *Ramayana* covered twenty-four recitals, each of which lasted about four hours. This legend which has been set down by numerous writers and sages, tells of the trials and final victory of the man-god Rama. The young prince and his wife Sita are banished from their country; while in the forests Sita is carried away by Ravana, the demon king of Lanka (Sri Lanka); Rama, with the help of his friends, notably the monkey god Hanuman and the monkey king Sugriva, crosses over to Lanka. He slays Ravana, rescues his wife and, after many mighty deeds, returns home a victor and is crowned. Into this story are interwoven many lessons to do with duty, honour, courage, truth and courtesy. In historical terms, of course, the epic justifies the Aryan incursions into south India but the Aryan Brahmins raised it to the status of a sacred text and it is as such that it is revered by millions in India. The righteous actions of the Aryan man-god Rama and his faithful wife Sita are pitted against the evil deeds of the Dravidian tyrant Ravana and his ilk and, in the end, the evil-doers are vanquished. Thus, over the ages, singers like Panchpakesa Bhagvatar have kept alive the race memory in India.

The *Mahabharata* contains frequent references to music and dance. This epic records the tribal wars of the Indian Aryans but, in the process of being transformed into a sacred work, it becomes a gigantic drama of good versus evil. It recounts the war of succession between the Kauravs and their cousins the Pandavs. The latter, being the rightful heirs, are the ones who are favoured by the god Krishna and are the final victors. Arjun, one of the Pandavs, has Krishna as his charioteer and counsellor during the decisive battle at Kurukshetra and it is here that Krishna delivers to Arjun the *Bhagavad Gita*, the Song Divine, which is the holiest book of the Hindus. The *Gita*, song, lays down the precepts of moral truth and right action and could be called, in all justice, 'the Hindu Bible'. Arjun, apart from being a mighty warrior, was also an expert musician and dancer and the *Mahabharata* tells us that he taught these arts to the Princess *Uttarā*.

By about 600 B.C. Sanskrit, the oldest known member of the Indo-European group of languages, had become firmly established as the sacred and literary language of India. It was at this time that the philosopher Panini wrote the world's first book on grammar and prosody. From the internal evidence in Panini's book it is clear that the allied arts of music, dance and drama had reached a sophisticated level in India. William Wilson Hunter, in his book *The Indian Empire*, states that a regular system of notation had been worked out before the time of Panini and that this notation "passed from the Brahmins through the Persians to Arabia, and was thence introduced into European music by Guido d'Arezzo at the beginning of the eleventh century." The Benedictine monk Guido is credited with having invented the stave, the 'Guidonian hand' to facilitate sight singing, as well as the ancestors of the sol-fa notes. If Hunter's theory is even partially correct, the Indian influence on the technical aspects of European music must have been not inconsiderable.

Apart from the religious and art music — the first confined to temple worship and the second to the courts — it would be well to remember that folk music was always a part of the day to day life of the common man. There were also troupes of travelling musicians, dancers and storytellers who, apart from performing their vital function of entertainment and instruction, kept open the lines of cultural communication between one part of the country and another. The word "country" is being used here very loosely and requires some explanation.

"India" is not an Indian word. Strictly speaking, neither is the word "Hindu" an Indian word. In none of the ancient, and not so ancient, texts do these words appear. The river Indus, which now flows through Pakistan, was known as "Sindhu" to the Aryans. This was later corrupted by the Persians and Greeks to "Indus"; the people living beyond the "Indus" were called "Hindus", and hence their "country" became "India". Thus "Indus", "Hindu" and "India" are foreign appellations. "Aryavarta" and, later, "Bharat" are the two names that the Aryans used for their "country" in which there were numerous kingdoms and republics but which had a common Aryanized, Vedic and Sanskritized culture. "Bharat", therefore, had connotations of culture rather than of political boundaries. In Hindi, the national language of India, "Bharat" is the word used. Even this, however, gained political recognition only in 1949 when it was written into the constitution of the present-day Republic of India. The constitution was drafted in English and the Fathers of the republic, knowing full well that "India" was not an "Indian" word, specified the country to which they were referring as "India, that is Bharat, shall be a Union of States."

Historically, however, "Bharat" was a cultural Common Market that extended over vast areas of land and sometimes over the seas as well.

In the fifth century B.C. there arose in north India a new religion which was very different from the Vedic religion of the past. It was founded by Prince Siddharata of the Sakya tribe which inhabited the border lands between India and Nepal. The Prince forsook riches and power to preach equality among all men and came to be known as Buddha or the Enlightened One and, in due course, his teaching spread to most of the countries of Asia. Buddhism's most ardent champion was the saintly emperor Ashoka the Great (3rd century B.C.) who sent missionaries to Lanka, Burma, Thailand and China.

The genesis and growth of Buddhism is a fascinating study. Essentially a puritanical religion, it was a reaction against ritualism and caste. It involved no gods and no elaborate worship of them. Buddhist monks and nuns took vows of poverty and chastity and devoted their lives to social service and education. The Brahmins, however, could not sit idly by and let their power over the people be swept away by this wave of dangerous egalitarianism, and after Ashoka's death Brahminism began to reassert itself. The method used to blunt the reforming zeal of Buddhism was a particularly clever one. The Brahmins simply admitted the Buddha into the Hindu pantheon as an avatar of the god Vishnu and this, over a long period of time, turned Buddhism into a sect of Hinduism.

At first Buddhism, being a type of protestantism, had little time for the arts but in its heyday it produced miracles of sculpture, painting, and architecture. The Buddhist religious singers, *vaitālikas*, invented distinct musical forms for men and women and developed the *kumbhasthūn*, a percussion instrument made by stretching leather over the mouth of an earthen pot.

Outside India the Buddhist influence was, in many ways, far more profound. The Essenes, the only Jewish sect which upheld non-violence and with whom Jesus is said to have spent some time, were quite probably influenced by this aspect of Buddhist philosophy; Buddhist carvings exist in Afghanistan and Soviet Russia; and classical dance-dramas in Japan and Korea still use Buddhist themes.

Throughout this time there were increasing commercial and cultural links between the various countries of Asia. With Alexander's invasion of India in 326 B.C., there began in north India an Indo-Hellenic school of art and it is quite probable that both Indian and Greek music affected each other. Those who believe that it was the Greeks who brought the light of culture to India are patently misguided. Equally misguided are those who inform the world that Alexander sent philosophers and artists from India back to his native Greece to instruct his barbaric compatriots. Both Greece and India had arrived at a high level of cultural development and a story based on historical fact will illustrate this. By his brilliant generalship Alexander had defeated Porus, the king of the Punjab. Everybody expected that the king, who had been taken prisoner, would appear before his conqueror with suitable humility. Porus, however, stood erect. He was proud and unbowed. Alexander asked him, "How do you expect me to treat you?" "As one king ought to treat another," replied Porus. On hearing this Alexander and his generals were astounded. Then the young conqueror's face broke into a

smile, for here he had seen honour in adversity. He embraced
Porus, set him free and concluded a treaty with him.

In the 6th century B.C. Pythagoras, who had worked out a
system for musical modes, advanced the science of
mathematics and expounded a theory concerning the
transmigration of the soul. Pythagoras lived and worked on the
very edge of Asia Minor or, more correctly, West Asia and it is
not unreasonable to assume that not only must he have
influenced the Asians but that he, in his turn, might well have
been influenced by them.

One of the greatest problems that confronts the scholar of
ancient India is the vexed question of dates. "The Hindus had
no sense of history," is too facile a statement. A people who
believed that a man's sojourn on earth was only a momentary
stage leading to another existence, simply regarded the
meticulous recording of the dates of events in this transient
episode as irrelevant. History, as we know it, is a Greek
invention. Perhaps scholars rely too much on precise dates. It
is, nevertheless, a great pity that no one can place in time —
with any degree of exactitude — the earliest musicologists of
India. The first of these was Narada who undertook the task of
finding a relationship between sacred and secular music. He
also discovered the features common to folk and art music.
Tradition has it that Narada was a sage, a *muni* who, after
accomplishing his work on earth, left for the Elysian fields
where he still plays his lute. To further complicate matters
later theorists took the cognomen 'Narada', so that we now
have four books by different Naradas. Research has,
nevertheless, proved that the first Narada was the author of
Sikṣā ('learning' or 'training'). This was the first work that
examined music in a spirit of scientific enquiry.

India's greatest writer on the arts, the sage Bharata, is also a
misty figure of antiquity. His book, the *Bharata Natya
Shastra*, was regarded as a sacred book and was called the
Fifth Veda. It was, and still is, the most important work on
Indian aesthetics and covers music, dance, drama and
criticism. European Sanskritists knew of the existence of this
book from references to it in various source material but
believed that all manuscripts had been lost or destroyed. It was
only in the latter half of the last century that, while working on

a mediaeval work on drama, Hall came across a manuscript of the *Natya Shastra*. Others were then discovered and much spadework was done by the German Heymann, and by the Frenchmen Regnaud, Grosset and Lévi. In 1894 Pandits Shivadatta and Kashinath Pandurang Parab published the original Sanskrit text and in 1950 Manomohan Ghosh made the first translation into English. Ghosh's treatment and translation of the *Natya Shastra* is a major work of scholarship and original research.

When Bharata was asked to explain the origins of his book, he replied that when the people of the world strayed from a righteous path "their happiness was mixed with sorrow". The gods then asked Brahma, the Great Father, to devise a new *Veda* which could be seen as well as heard and which would belong to all the people. Brahma, therefore, agreed to create the Fifth Veda which would induce "duty, wealth, as well as fame, and contain good counsel ...", which would be "enriched by the teaching of all the scriptures and give a review of all arts and crafts". So Brahma took recitation from the *Rig-Veda*, song from the *Sam-Veda*, histrionic representation from the *Yajur-Veda* and the sentiments from the *Atharva-Veda*, and with a combination of these created the new *Veda*.

Brahma then asked the god Indra to teach it to the other gods, but Indra said that the gods would neither understand nor interpret the *Veda* skillfully enough. He suggested instead, that the sages were better fitted to receive the new scripture. Brahma, therefore, taught the *Veda* to Bharata who, in turn, instructed his hundred 'sons', by which is probably meant men who followed him in becoming authorities on music, dance and drama.

These 'sons' of Bharata have been the cause of much confusion. Many musicologists after Bharata used his surname and so we have Ādi-Bharata, Kohala-Bharata, Matanga-Bharata, and Nandikeshvara-Bharata.

The date and authorship of the *Bharata Natya Shastra* are both in dispute. The book has been variously dated from the 2nd century B.C. to the 3rd century A.D., but there is even less certainty about the author. However, let us examine the corpus of the work itself.

Bharata conceived of all art as a whole. There was, for him, an essential unity of all artistic forms. This idea coincides with one of Hinduism's basic tenets that there is a fundamental unity in all diversity. The *Natya Shastra* makes the close relationship of music, dance, drama and painting very clear indeed. There is a lesson in the story that tells of a king who wanted to make sculptures of the gods and who went to a sage for instruction. "You will have to learn the laws of painting before you can understand the laws of sculpture", said the sage. "Then", said the king, "teach me the laws of painting." "It is not possible to understand the laws of painting," replied the sage, "without learning the art of dance." "So instruct me in the art of dance." "That would be difficult," said the sage, "as you do not know the principles of instrumental music". The king was, by now, getting impatient. "Then why don't you teach me instrumental music?" he demanded hastily. "But you cannot understand instrumental music," answered the sage, "without a thorough study of vocal music, for vocal music is the source of all the arts." The king then bent low and begged the sage to instruct him in vocal music.

Since musical notes were first produced by the human throat, it is natural that Bharata and those who followed him should have emphasized the pre-eminence of vocal music. They believed that the first instrument available to Man was the human voice which produced the primal notes and that therefore all man-made instruments should imitate or emulate the human voice. For them the purest and highest type of music was that which took its example from the human voice and which thus worked on the principle of one note at a time. Over the centuries India has retained this principle and has developed, within its framework, a highly complicated and sophisticated system of modal music.

Bharata said that it was the musician-composer's business — as, indeed, of every artist — to evoke a particular emotion or mood which he called *rasa*. He enumerated eight such emotional states and gave to each a presiding deity and a colour equivalent.

Some later authorities mention a ninth *rasa*, Shanta or serenity. The presiding deity here is Narayana and the colour is the white of the lightly fragrant kunda flower. These

Name of Rasa	Nearest equivalent	Deity	Colour
Shringar	Love	Vishnu	Light green
Hasya	Humour	Pramatha	White
Karuna	Pathos	Yama	Ash
Rudra	Anger	Rudra	Red
Vir	Heroism	Indra	Light orange
Bhayanaka	Terror	Kala	Black
Bibhatsa	Disgust	Shiva as Mahakala	Blue
Adbhuta	Wonder	Brahma	Yellow

Nava-rasas, nine basic emotions, are fundamental to Indian aesthetics.

The musician was to use *swaras,* musical notes, as the poet words, the sculptor stone or the dancer movement. Each in his own way had to evoke *rasa.* The *Natya Shastra* sets down rules and makes suggestions so that the creative artist achieves this end. The book is as significant in India as Aristotle's *Poetics* is in the West.

The *saptak,* the seven notes of the scale, was established by the time Bharata wrote his book. The seven notes were classified as: Sadja, Risabha, Gandhara, Madhyama, Panchama, Dhaivata, Nishada. They are known by the initial sounds of their names: SA, RE, GA, MA, PA, DHA, NI. In the Western scale they correspond to C, D, E, F, G, A, B. In mythology the *swaras* were associated with the sounds of birds and animals:

SA — the peacock's cry.
RE — the cow calling her calf.
GA — the goat's bleat.
MA — the heron's cry.
PA — the cuckoo's song.
DHA — the horse's neigh.
NI — the elephant's trumpeting.

Bharata noted that there were twenty-two intervals in a *saptak*. These microtonal intervals he called *srutis,* and these were spread over the *swaras* in a very special way.

There were three parent scales or *gramas* in India even before Bharata's time. These were *Sadja-grama, Madhyama-grama,* and *Gandhara-grama.* The *Gandhara-grama* had become obsolete by the time of the *Natya Shastra* and so Bharata did not describe it. In the *Sadja-grama* the *srutis* were as follows: three in RE, two in GA, four in MA, four in PA, three in DHA, two in NI, and four in SA. In the *Madhyama-grama* the *srutis* were: four in MA, three in PA, four in DHA, two in NI, four in SA, three in RE, and two in GA. Each of these two *gramas* was the source of seven *murchanas* or modes.

SADJA-GRAMA

Name of *murchana*	Order of *swaras*	Greek modal equivalent
Uttaramandra	SA—RE—GA—MA—PA—DHA—NI	Ionian
Rajani	RE—GA—MA—PA—DHA—NI—SA	Dorian
Uttarayata	GA—MA—PA—DHA—NI—SA—RE	Phrygian
Suddhasadja	MA—PA—DHA—NI—SA—RE—GA	Lydian
Asvakranta	PA—DHA—NI—SA—RE—GA—MA	Mixolydian
Matsarikrta	DHA—NI—SA—RE—GA—MA—PA	Aeolian
Abhirudgata	NI—SA—RE—GA—MA—PA—DHA	—

The question that arises is: what was the essential difference between *Sadja-grama* and *Madhyama-grama?* It was, in effect, a technical one to do with microtonal intervals (*srutis*): in *Sadja-grama* PA (G) had four *srutis* and DHA (A) three *srutis,* whereas in *Madhyama-grama* PA had three and DHA four. The first note of the first *murchana* in *Sadja-grama* was SA and the first note of the first *murchana* in *Madhyama-grama* was MA. For the musicians of that time this may have served a functional purpose.

The fourteen *murchanas* that we have named were of a heptatonic character. There were also some hexatonic

MADHYAMA-GRAMA

Name of *murchana*	Order of *swaras*	Greek modal equivalent
Sauviri	MA—PA—DHA—NI—SA—RE—GA	Lydian
Harinasva	PA—DHA—NI—SA—RE—GA—MA	Mixolydian
Kalopanata	DHA—NI—SA—RE—GA—MA—PA	Aeolian
Suddhamadhya	NI—SA—RE—GA—MA—PA—DHA	—
Margavi	SA—RE—GA—MA—PA—DHA—NI	Ionian
Pauravi	RE—GA—MA—PA—DHA—NI—SA	Dorian
Hirsyaka	GA—MA—PA—DHA—NI—SA—RE	Phrygian

murchanas, pentatonic *murchanas* and those which had overlapping notes. To these Bharata gave the name *'tanas'*.

Nowhere did Bharata use the word *raga*. He did, however, use the word *jati* which to him meant a melody archetype. He recognized eighteen *jatis* of two kinds: *suddha*, the pure and *vikrit*, the modified. There were seven *suddha jatis* and eleven *vikrit jatis*. Four of the *suddha jatis* were in *Sadja-grama* and three in *Madhyama-grama*. Of the ten characteristics of each *jati* the most important were *graha* (clef), *amsa* (keynote) and *nyasa* (cadence).

Bharata's treatise is remarkable for its hair-splitting analysis. He examined the inherent qualities of the *swaras* in detail and recommended their particular uses. The note MA, for example, evoked the erotic sentiment. DHA, when used as an *amsa*, evoked terror and GA as an *amsa* evoked pathos. After studying the notes in isolation he went on to various combinations of notes in their ascending and descending orders.

The sage was fully aware of the importance of instrumental music, for although he believed that vocal music was prior to instrumental music, he also realized that the scientific investigation of music began only when musical instruments reached a particular stage of development. The *veena*, a lute

sacred to Saraswati, the goddess of learning and the fine arts,
played a crucial part in this investigation. Bharata, therefore,
gave careful instructions about the playing of this instrument
and it emerges that the *veena* of Bharata's time was very
different from today's *veena*. After his discourse on stringed
instruments Bharata went on to wind and percussion
instruments.

The importance of the *Natya Shastra* cannot be overstated
and there will be further references to this book later.

Bharata was followed by a host of theorists who built up a
most distinguished body of musicology. There was Visavasu
(about the 2nd century A.D.) who studied the *sruti* and
Nandikeshvara, of approximately the same period, who wrote
about a type of twelve note *murchana*. This Nandikeshvara
might well have been the same critic who produced the
Abhinaya Darpanam, a classic on the facial expressions and
gestures of dance. A number of authors also contributed to two
compilations, the *Markandeya-purana* and the *Vayu-purana*.
The first dates from the 3rd century A.D. and deals with the
content and form of songs. The second provides a
comprehensive picture of the state of music under the Gupta
dynasty during the 4th century A.D.

After the Guptas two changes are discernible. First, the idea
of the *raga* started to take shape. Second, throughout the
subcontinent a number of regional languages began to gain a
respectable identity. Sanskrit was still the language of higher
learning and discourse, the sacred tongue, as was Latin in
Europe. Nonetheless, the *desa-bhasa* or 'country languages'
had started to challenge the cultural authority of Sanskrit.
One reads, for instance, that in the 6th century A.D. the poet
Isana was recognized as a *bhasa-kavi*, that is, one who wrote
poetry in a regional language. Now if religious verses were
being written in *desa-bhasa* it follows that the style of the
musical compositions that would carry those verses would also
have to be altered. Matanga, Yastika, Kashyapa, Durgashakti
and Banabhatta — all music critics of that time — wrote about
these new types or styles of music quite extensively. The music
was essentially the same, in that it was founded on the *raga*
system which had descended from the *jatis* of Bharata's time,
but with regional variations dependent upon diversities of

language, climate and temperament. It was from these early times, therefore, that the classical music of India — one still in spirit and form — began to move in the different stylistic directions which eventually stabilised into two great styles. The Islamic influence, which was felt much later, certainly helped towards this stabilisation but the process had begun very much earlier. India was aware of and in touch with the cultures of Greece, West Asia, China, Rome and Persia long before the birth of Islam, and because of geographical proximity the northern part of the subcontinent was, naturally, more open to such contacts.

The Greeks had their modes, the Persians their *dastgahs*, the Arabs their *maqams* and the Indians their *ragas*. Is it a mere coincidence that all these were melodic, non-harmonic, types of music? It is idle chauvinism to speculate as to which was more indebted to the other. Three facts, however, need to be pointed out: (i) The Indian *ragas* have always been closely associated with religious practises, (ii) when this music was used for secular purposes it retained its profound and spiritual nature, (iii) the *raga* system has developed continually over the centuries and is today India's main 'cultural export'. Only that art form which is firmly rooted in Nature and all its manifestations, which evokes the innermost yearnings of the spirit and mind of Man, and which is supported by a solid foundation of theory, can hope to survive down through the ages. That the *raga* system of India is one such art form is beyond dispute.

The first text to discuss the *ragas* in detail was the *Brihaddesi*, written in the 9th century and ascribed to Matanga. The name of this work is significant for it derives from *desi*, or *desa-bhasa* meaning 'country languages'. This reinforces the theory that the development and diversity of both language and music occurred simultaneously.

We now come to a time in India's history when precise dating becomes possible.

2   Music and Dance in the Temples

India was the Holy Land for devout Buddhists in China and south-east Asia and many of them made pilgrimages to the country of Buddha's birth. In his account of his travels in India the seventh century Chinese pilgrim Huien Tsang has left a vivid description of the country. He was followed by the Muslim historians Al-Djahiz (9th century), Al-Masudi (10th century) and Al-Biruni (11th century). The last of these, Al-Biruni, is a great historical figure and he studied the Indian subcontinent very closely for a period of twelve years. At the age of forty-five he mastered Sanskrit and translated Euclid's *Elements* and his own treatise on astronomy into that language. He then embarked upon the translation of the Indian literary classic *Panchatantra* into Arabic. Al-Biruni's greatest work, however, was his *India* in which he quoted twenty-four works by fourteen Greek writers and used forty Sanskrit sources. He was the first foreign scholar to write on India with vast knowledge and deep understanding.

These Muslims, who had no religious affiliations with the Indians, could study Indian music objectively and they formed a favourable opinion of it. This, in spite of the fact that music and dance had by this time come to be associated with temple prostitution.

Now the phenomenon of temple prostitution was not unique to India. This was because the Mother Goddess, connected with the fertility cult, appears in all ancient civilizations under different names: Mylitta, Isis, Aphrodite, Venus, Parvati and Ceres to name only a few. The gift most acceptable to the goddess was the virginity of a girl since the female sex organs were a symbol of fertility and prosperity. Herodotus records sacred fertility cult prostitution in Assyria and Cyprus. St. Augustine writes of a custom in Phoenicia where parents offered their virgin daughters to the temple of Venus to be prostituted in the service of the goddess. Lucian says that at the great temple to Venus at Byblos he saw women mourning the death of Adonis by shaving off their hair. Those among them who were unwilling to sacrifice their hair were allowed, instead, to sell themselves for a day and pay their earnings into the temple funds.

There is ample evidence in the writings of Socrates, Apollodorus, Plautus, Justin, Eusebius and others which tells of sacred prostitution in Egypt, Greece, West Asia and North Africa.

In India the worship of Surya, who was the equivalent of Apollo, required the services of girls in the temples to sing and dance in honour of the god. The *Padmapurana* recommended the dedication of girls to the temple of Surya as one of the surest ways of gaining Suryaloka, the heaven of the sun-god. The fact that the gods were accustomed to having *apsaras*, celestial nymphs, to sing and dance for them in heaven gave divine sanction to this statement. The recommendation was obviously implemented by the worshippers of Surya for Huien Tsang writes about the large number of sacred prostitutes at the temple of Surya in Multan, in north India, now in Pakistan.

When the great temples were built in India, girls trained in music and dance were attached to them as a matter of course. These not only sang and danced before the idol, but also provided income for the shrine. The ninth and tenth centuries saw the most glorious period of temple architecture and it was at this time that the temples of south India, still famous today, were built.

The richness of the decoration of these temples was beautifully complemented by the enchanting forms of the temple prostitutes or *devadasis*, literally handmaidens of the gods. We know from inscriptions that Rajaraja, the Chola king, had four hundred *devadasis* installed in his temple at Tanjore. They lived in luxury in the streets surrounding the temple and were granted tax-free lands. The high regard in which these women were held was not at all surprising, for they were educated, skilled in languages and experts in music and dance. Moreover, they were 'married' to the temple deity.

The 'marriage' rituals varied from region to region. In the Coimbatore area at least one girl from each family of musicians was selected for temple service. She was usually the most beautiful and talented girl in the family. After some initial training at home she was dressed in fine clothes and bedecked with jewels. She was made to stand on a heap of rice (a fertility symbol) and two *devadasis*, also standing on heaps of rice, held a folded cloth before her. The girl then held the cloth while her teacher grasped her ankles and moved them up and down in time to music. In the evening she was taken to the temple for the *tali* (wedding necklace) tying ceremony. She was made to sit in front of the idol and the priest gave her flowers and marked her forehead with sandalwood paste. He then tied the *tali*, which lay at the idol's feet, round her neck. She then commenced her arduous training in music and dance, and when she reached the proper age she was deflowered by a Brahmin priest who represented the god.

Among the Basava sub-caste the girl was 'married' in a similar fashion, but to a dagger. This was clearly a phallic symbol representing the *lingam*, penis, of the god Shiva. At the Suchindram temple in south Travancore the 'marriage' of the idol to the *devadasi* was symbolic of the marriage of Shiva to his consort Parvati.

Since the *devadasi* was 'married' to a god she could never be a widow, and so she was considered lucky. Her presence, therefore, on occasions such as weddings and births was considered essential. Whenever possible she made *talis* for others and sometimes incorporated a bead or two from her own as a special favour.

We have two descriptions of the temple courtesans in the Vijayanagar empire from dependable foreign observers. The first is Domingo Paes, who was a member of the Portuguese Embassy. He says that any high-born man might visit these ladies without censure, that they lived in the best quarters of the city, and were permitted to sit and even chew betel in the presence of the King's wives. Seeing them on one particular occasion he writes: "Who can describe the treasure these women carry on their persons? ... There are some among them who have had lands presented to them and litters and maidservants without number." The murals of a temple near Conjeevaram authenticate Paes' observations. Fernao Nuniz, a countryman of Paes, writes about the *devadasis* in similar terms.

Methwold, who visited the Muslim kingdom of Golconda during the time of Elizabeth I, remarks that these ladies, "whom the lawes of the country do both allow and protect", were invited to formal public functions. They were present at circumcisions, weddings, ships' arrivals and private feasts and were "paid for their company".

The mention of circumcision is significant for this is a Muslim religious ritual. It means that even the Muslims had by then accepted the Hindu temple courtesans as harbingers of good fortune.

During Muslim rule in north India the courtesans of Agra, Delhi and Lucknow were justly famous for their culture and refinement. Mundy, an English traveller, informs us that there were various types of *tavaifs*, courtesans, and they were regarded as distinct from the level of common prostitutes. The sons of the upper classes were sent to the *tavaifs* in order to round off their education. This used to happen even in the early decades of this century and some of the most eminent men in politics, law, and letters have in the recent past imbibed their culture from the *tavaifs*. Though most of these *tavaifs* were Muslims and so had no connection with temples, their development obviously owes much to the *devadasis*. Their accomplishments, particularly in music and dancing, were equal to those of the *devadasis* and their 'marriage' to trees and flowering plants compare exactly with the customs of the temple courtesans.

The social customs of south India at the end of the eighteenth century are fully described by the Abbé Dubois. He was well qualified to write *Hindu Manners, Customs and Ceremonies*, since he had spent thirty years of his life in India. Writing about the status of women in general, he says that it was not considered seemly for ordinary women to learn to read, sing or dance. If any of them did by chance acquire any of these skills then, far from exhibiting them, they would be ashamed to own up to them. This attitude was fostered by the fact that only the *devadasis* required the use of these arts.

The *devadasis* had a reputation for bringing good luck and the abbé says that it was considered most improper to go anywhere without a number of these attendant 'good luck charms'. What surprised him most of all was the modesty of these women. He admires their good taste in clothes and the civility of their language. "Indeed," he says, "they are particularly careful not to expose any part of their body." With the understanding worthy of an educated Frenchman he concludes that this probably arises from their sophistication in the art of seduction, the unseen being more tantalizing than the seen.

In 1870 Dr. Shortt, a surgeon who had worked in south India, delivered a lecture on the subject of the *devadasis* to the Anthropological Society of London. He, like the Abbé Dubois, praised their beauty and culture and said that many European officers had taken them for mistresses.

In the early years of this century Thurston encountered many *devadasis* in the temples of Madurai, Conjeevaram and Tanjore. In his *Castes and Tribes of Southern India* he tells how a *devadasi* retired from her profession. First she had to apply to the temple authorities for 'permission to remove her ear-pendants' which meant that she wished to retire. The retirement ceremony then took place in the Maharaja's palace: "At the appointed spot the officers concerned assemble, and the woman, seated on a wooden plank, proceeds to unhook the pendants, and places them, with a *nuzzar* (gift) of twelve *fanams* (coins) on the plank. Directly after this she turns about, and walks away without casting a second glance at the ear ornaments which have been laid down. She becomes immediately a *taikkizhavi* or old woman, and is supposed to lead a life of retirement and resignation." The pendants were later returned to her, but she never wore them again.

In the Princely States of south India the rights and status of the *devadasis* were recognized and safeguarded, and they had the same rights in British India in all areas under the jurisdiction of the Madras High Court. Their way of life was based on matrilineal law and property generally passed from mother to daughter. Although connected with the temples, they were not Brahmins. They formed, as it were, a caste unto themselves. The daughters of *devadasis* followed their mothers' profession and the sons became *nattuvanars*, musicians, and dance teachers. Many *nattuvanars* took the surname Pillai or Mudali, which were regarded as respectable adjuncts to a name. These musicians and dance teachers have jealously guarded and preserved the art of music and dance through the centuries. Many of them were illiterate and so had no access to the literature connected with the arts. However, some families tenaciously held on to the theoretical background and set a standard for both the practice and theory of music and dance. Particular mention must be made of the great musician Mattuswami Dikshitar and his pupils, the brothers Chinniyah, Punniah, Shivanandan and Vadivelu Pillai. They, their families, and their pupils have helped to keep alive the highest traditions right up to the present time.

Victorian missionary ladies were absolutely shocked and appalled at what they encountered in south India. Pressure was brought to bear upon the British administrators and the Indian princes that temple prostitution be stopped. The missionaries were not alone in this crusade, for many western-educated Indians too joined the hue and cry against the *devadasis*. Mysore State stopped the dedication of *devadasis* in 1910 and Travancore State did likewise in 1930. In 1927, however, there were still 200,000 temple prostitutes in Madras Presidency alone, which was part of British India. In that same year Gandhi wrote, "There are, I am sorry to say, many temples in our midst in this country which are no better than brothels."

Katherine Mayo, in her books *Mother India* (1927) and *Slaves of the Gods* (1929), presented a false and one-sided view of Indian society, but she succeeded, nevertheless, in bringing the evils of the *devadasi* system to the notice of people in India and abroad; for there can be no doubt that by the early decades of this century the institution of *devadasis* had degenerated to mass prostitution on an unprecedented scale and served only to make the Brahmin custodians of the temples richer and more corrupt. But how did this degeneration take place? We must remember that, since they were not Brahmins, successive generations of *devadasi* families were deprived of formal education and this meant that their position in the caste hierarchy dropped lower and lower. Thus, as a caste, they were open to exploitation and abuse. The impact of western liberalism and technology, which came with British rule, reduced spiritual fervour, with the result that the arts and artists associated with the temple were neglected. The western-educated Indians, already mentioned, formed the so-called 'enlightened class' of the country and it was they who had lost sight of the true value of their heritage and allowed it to deteriorate. This was probably partly due to their eagerness to precipitate themselves into the modern age and partly perhaps because they were dazzled by the new western culture.

Although there are no *devadasis* as such in India today, there are many good musicians, dancers and dance teachers who come from *devadasi* families. It is these families which, in spite of humiliation and poverty in the past, have kept alive the cultural heritage of India.

The *devadasis* and *nattuvanars* had their counterparts in north India in the *tavaifs, bais,* and *ustads.* They too have been through dark periods in the not too distant past. Today, however, a whole generation after Independence, a massive rehabilitation has taken place. *Devadasis* have become "Shrimati-jis" (the honorific for respectable married ladies), *nattuvanars* have become "Guru-jis" (respected teachers), *tavaifs* have become "Begums" (noble ladies), *bais* have become "Devis" (akin to goddesses — the word is related to *dea* and *diva*), and the *ustads* have become "Khan Sahibs" (the honorific for Muslim gentlemen of high rank). There has been a proliferation of "Pandits" as well. This word, which is now commonly used in English for political forecasters and experts of all kinds, was originally used as a term of respect for members of the Brahmin caste — hence 'Pandit Nehru'. In addition, musicians and other performing artists have been awarded national honours by the state. Now all this — which does seem a trifle selfconscious — is a happy trend and should continue. No country in the world can encourage its artists too much.

Now that Indian music has become more secular, and therefore more democratic, two changes are noticeable. Firstly, there has emerged in India the purely concert hall artist; and secondly, a large number of musicians are coming from the middle class, a class which previously had no connection with music. Both these changes will be considered in a later chapter.

Balasaraswati, widely regarded as the last of the great *devadasis*.
Courtesy: Nala Najan

A rare photograph of a *devadasi* during the early years of this century. *Courtesy: Nala Najan*

Two well known *devadasis* of the 1930s: *Saranayaki* (left) and *Pattu* were trained by Vadivelu Pillai, a member of the 'Thanjavur Quartette'. *Courtesy: Nala Najan*

3 Many Peoples, many Songs

Before one can aspire to any understanding of the creative impulses of the inhabitants of the India-Pakistan-Bangladesh subcontinent, it is as well to know something about its vast conglomerate of peoples. India, for example, has 845 languages and dialects. This alone will convey some idea of the diversity to be apprehended.

How did this diversity come about?

Mention has already been made of the Indus Valley civilization during the pre-Vedic era (6000-2500 B.C.). Flourishing at the same time were the Sumerian civilization in the Tigris-Euphrates basin and the Egyptian civilization in the Nile basin. These three cultures formed what is known as the Fertile Crescent. We know that they traded with each other and that jade from Central Asia was sent from Kashgar down to Mohenjo Daro, and thence across Persia to Ur in Sumer and Memphis in Egypt.

The Aryans entered the subcontinent around 2000 B.C. probably through the Malakand and Khyber Passes. They came in successive waves and by 800 B.C. had established themselves as far east as the river Brahmaputra. They brought with them the Vedic age. This means that the great religious literature of India that started with the *Rig-Veda* and the predominant religion of India, Hinduism, are both foreign in origin. Hindu extremists in India today would do well to consider this fact.

With the Aryans came the institution of caste. The Aryans themselves, who were the rulers and fair-skinned, became the higher castes. The indigenous inhabitants, who were dark, either became the lower castes or isolated themselves in hilly areas and forests. It is interesting that the Sanskrit word *varna* means both caste and colour.

The Aryan expansion into south India was checked by the mountain ranges and dense forests which extended across central India. However, Aryan sages and missionaries spread into the whole of Dravida, south India, and converted the inhabitants to the Aryan way of life. These sages and missionaries, with their families, formed the nucleus of the south Indian Brahmin castes. Knowing that they were surrounded by a sea of dark, hostile Dravidians, these south Indian Brahmins have always preserved their identity more fanatically than their Brahmin brothers in the north. Their situation, in fact, was analogous to that of the whites in southern Africa today. To this day the Madras Brahmins pride themselves on their exclusiveness and the fairness of their skin.

The Aryan Brahmins monopolised all learning and developed a facility for coexisting with the lower castes on the basis of their own superiority. They were an elitist class who were in a position to manipulate the power of state and religion in order to maintain Brahminic ascendancy. They provided the philosophers, the chief ministers, the diplomats, the high priests and, sometimes, even the generals. The breakaway or reformist movements, therefore, were mainly inspired and led by non-Brahmins. The Buddha who founded Buddhism, Mahavira who founded Jainism and Guru Nanak who founded Sikhism were all born Kshatriyas. Mahatma Gandhi was born a Vaishya.

The Brahmin gods were mostly fair-skinned but one of the notable exceptions was Krishna, the Dark One, who represented a major concession by the Aryan Brahmins to their dark-skinned compatriots. He was always depicted as a charming young man with a flute, whose ethereal music melted the heart of every maiden. Krishna is a popular god in India for, in sociological terms, he has become a bridge between the Aryan and the Dravidian cultures.

In the 6th century B.C. Persia established a powerful empire and Darius annexed Sind and the western Punjab. These areas remained a part of the Persian empire up to the time that it was overthrown by Alexander in 330 B.C. The rest of the subcontinent was divided up into kingdoms, principalities and republics. The chief kingdoms in the north were Magadha, Anga, Kosala, Vatsa and Avanti; in the Deccan plateau were Andhra and Kalinga; and in the south there were the Chola, the Pandya and the Kerala kingdoms.

After Alexander's death his kingdom was parcelled out among his generals. It was at this time that the Mauryan empire took back the Indian territories from the Greeks and pushed its frontier to the Hindu Kush. The Mauryans controlled a large part of the subcontinent from their capital in Taxila, now in Pakistan. Nevertheless, the Chola, the Pandya and the Kerala kingdoms in the south were independent of them and the Andhra kingdom in the Deccan was probably an independent state within the empire.

The kingdom of Kerala, on the south-west coast of India had, all this time, been trading with the Phoenicians and the Greeks by sea. From the time of Augustus the Romans also started trading with Kerala via Alexandria and the Red Sea. During the reign of Claudius the monsoon winds were harnessed to aid navigation and this helped the development of the international trade. The Romans came to Kerala for spices, hardwood, gold, peacocks, apes and ivory. After the second sack of Jerusalem many Jews sought refuge here and a colony settled in Cochin. There is also, in Kerala, a large community of Christians who take pride in the ancient origin of their Church and claim that it was founded by St. Thomas.

With the fall of the Mauryan empire in about 180 B.C. northern India was conquered by four different peoples and each of them settled there. The Greeks from Bactria, known to Indians as the Yavanas, held sway for about fifty years; the Pallavas and Sakas from central Asia ruled for about two hundred years; and the Yue-chi under Kanishka established the Kushan empire that lasted for over a hundred and fifty years. The racial and linguistic mixture was becoming very complex but this was not, by any means, the end.

The Gupta dynasty now established an empire that covered a large part of north India. From 300-500 A.D. there was a period of comparative peace and the arts flourished; the *Vayu-purana* was compiled during this time. The Deccan and south Indian had once more regrouped into different states.

The Tamil language of south India had reached full maturity by now for in the second century Ilango Adigal had written *Silappadikaram*, the "Epic of the Anklet", which is a classic of that language.

The Hindu colonisation of Java, Sumatra, Cambodia and Malaya had started in the first century and this continued for a long time. The colonists were chiefly from the east coast of India and from what is now Bengal and Bangladesh.

The Huns from central Asia were now threatening the whole of the civilized world. Under Attila they crossed the Rhine and were soon exacting tribute from the Roman empire. Another horde, the White Huns, over-ran Persia and entered India. They destroyed the Gupta empire and established themselves under their rulers Toramana and Mihiragula. At the beginning of the seventh century Harsha, who had led the Indian princes in their confrontation with the Huns, united most of north India. Harsha's plans, however, to bring the whole of the country under one rule were frustrated by the powerful Chalukyas of the Deccan, who stopped him at the Vindhya mountains. In the south the Pallavas were the paramount power and there was constant warfare between them and their neighbours, the Chalukyas.

After the collapse of Harsha's empire the map of India was very confused indeed. In the Punjab was the kingdom of Jayapala; in the centre was the Prathihara empire comprising a number of Rajput clans (descendants of the Gurjaras who had invaded India after the Huns); in the east were the Palas; in the Deccan the Chalukyas were being challenged by the Rashtrakutas; to the east of the Deccan there was the Kalinga kingdom; and in the south the Pallavas had collapsed and the Cholas were back in power.

While India was undergoing these long periods of disunity and political rivalry a new force had arisen in the deserts of Arabia. Islam was a strong monotheistic religion as well as a social and political philosophy. Within a short time the petty warring Arab tribes had been welded into a powerful nation. Being a daughter religion of Judaism and Christianity, Islam sanctioned the use of military force for the attainment of religious and political ends. At Qadesiyeh in 636 A.D. the Arabs destroyed the Persian empire and a century later they entered India. They crossed the Indus and settled in Sind as their advance further eastwards was checked by the Rajputs in the Thar desert.

This was not, however, India's first contact with Islam. Arab traders had already started trade with the Malabar coast of Kerala and a number of Arabs had settled there. There was, nevertheless, one vital difference: whereas in north India the Arabs were rulers, in Kerala they were traders. It is interesting to see that for two hundred years — from the 8th to the 10th centuries — the Muslims made no further territorial gains in India. In fact, during this time, the Indian states had the most cordial relations with the Abbassid empire which was ruled from Baghdad. In music the cultural exchange is exemplified by the names of two *ragas, Yemani* and *Kafi*, which clearly indicate Arabic origins. In mathematics, the Arabs took their numerals from India (the Arabic word for numerals is 'Hindsa', meaning 'from India'). Of course, when Europe adopted 'Arabic' numerals it was not realized that these were 'Indian' numerals.

After the Turks had dominated the Abbassid empire they commenced the invasion of India. It was they who started a permanent Muslim settlement in India during the eleventh century. These Muslims were of differing racial stock — Arabs, Turks, Persians, Afghans, and Mongols. All brought with them their own contributions to the multi-coloured fabric of Indian society. Even though they were of the same religion, their cultural and political interests were often at variance. This is seen from the history of over four hundred years of Muslim power in the subcontinent prior to the Mughal invasion. Indeed the Mughals, who were Muslims of Mongol origin although of Persian culture, wrested the Indian empire from their co-religionists rather than from the Hindus.

The Mughals brought most of the subcontinent under one central authority and the greatest of them, Akbar, who was a contemporary of Elizabeth I, made a genuine attempt to bring about a synthesis of the Hindu and Muslim religions.

Never were religions more different than Hinduism and Islam. Hinduism had evolved over the ages, Islam was a revealed religion; Hinduism was polytheistic, Islam was emphatically monotheistic; Hinduism had engendered an elaborate system of castes and sub-castes, Islam preached that all men were brothers; Hinduism saw many paths to God, Islam only one; Hinduism encouraged the making of idols, Islam was iconoclastic; Hinduism was non-prosleytizing, Islam was the opposite; Hindus venerated the cow, the Muslims ate it. The list can go on for pages. For over a millennium, in spite of the many invasions, Hindu society had not been challenged in this way. Islam too had never before encountered such a bewildering number of problems. Both religions had now to adjust to an entirely new situation. This adjustment found expression in many ways. The Bhagti movement, for instance, stressed the brotherhood of man irrespective of religion or social background. It combined the most attractive features of both Hinduism and Islam and produced saints like Kabir (1440-1518) who, though born a Muslim, renounced formal Islam and became the generative source of great poetry and music. Bhagti encouraged mysticism as did Sufism, which was a pantheistic type of Islam, and both relied heavily on the use of music.

It was the tremendous influence of Sufi thought throughout the Islamic world that directly influenced the later Muslim monarchs in India to encourage and even foster the Hindu arts.

Nevertheless, it would be an exaggeration to assume that there was complete Hindu-Muslim integration in India. Integration is a fashionable concept today but not necessarily a wholly desirable objective. The subcontinent is the richer and the more fascinating for the many kinds of people that inhabit it. The wider the variety of birds in a garden the more varied the song.

4 Musical Concourse

Against the social, political and religious background of the last chapter we can continue with the history of Indian musicology after the tenth century.

In 1919 a rare manuscript was discovered at Gadwal which then lay within the dominions of the Nizam of Hyderabad. On the recommendation of the British Resident in Hyderabad the local ruler, the Raja of Gadwal, permitted R.A.K. Shastry of the Baroda Central Library to study the manuscript. Later, the document was published under the auspices of the Maharaja of Baroda. This was the *Sangeet-makaranda* written by Narada in the eleventh century. Quite obviously this Narada was not the author of *Sikṣā*. The *Sangeet-makaranda* has proved to be a useful book for the dating and evaluation of other works of this period. It was also used by the renowned Sarangadeva two centuries later.

During the twelfth century Bengal produced two outstanding talents in the sphere of music criticism and poetry. Locana-kavi, the musician at the court of King Vallalasena, completed his *Raga-tarangini* in 1160. He recognized twelve basic *ragas* upon which eighty-six derivative *ragas* were built. We know that Locana-kavi wrote other books as well but these seem to have been either lost or destroyed. Jayadeva, the celebrated poet of the *Gita Govinda*, was born a few years after Locana-kavi. He was a poet-musician of the Vaishnavite cult which emphasized the worship of Vishnu, the god of preservation in the Hindu triad. Vishnu's incarnation, Krishna, now became the subject of much music and dance. In fact, all Indian art of this time was dominated by the Krishna theme. Krishna was a very human god and his romantic love for Radha symbolized the love of God for Man in terms which were simple and immediate.

As a child, Krishna was both naughty and precocious and was constantly annoying his foster-mother Yasoda by playing tricks on her. He was particularly fond of milk and butter and would lead raiding parties into the kitchen and larder. Yasoda once thought that he was eating mud and caught him roughly to open his mouth, but when she looked into the child's mouth she saw not mud but the entire earth with all its deep mysteries. As a young man Krishna's interests turned to milkmaids. There are numerous tales of his dalliances with the *gopees*, maidens, in the glades of Vrindaban by the banks of the sacred river Yamuna. As Murli Manohar or Govinda (flute playing cowherd) he would steal their affections by the magic of his divine music. Once while they were bathing in the river, Krishna hid their clothes and enjoyed their confusion from the vantage point of a tree-top. The chief target of the god's attentions, however, was the beautiful Radha and he would take every opportunity of teasing her in the presence of her friends by his flirtatious behaviour. Radha, of course, was passionately in love with Krishna and her heartbroken outpourings were, to the Vaishnavites, the soul's call to the infinite.

Jayadeva expressed all these Radha-Krishna episodes in erotic Sanskrit verse and specified the *tala*, rhythm, in which each section was to be sung and danced. He himself sang the verses and his wife, who was an expert dancer, interpreted them in dance form. In character and feeling the *Gita Govinda* has been compared with the Song of Solomon. It was published as *The Indian Song of Songs* when Sir Edwin Arnold translated it into English many years ago.

After Jayadeva the poet-musicians Chandidas, Tulsidas, Mira, Vidyapati and Surdas carried on the Vaishnavite tradition.

Sarangadeva (1210-1247) occupies a most important place in Indian music. A Brahmin from Kashmir in the far north of India, he lived in Daulatabad (formerly Deogiri) which is in the Deccan. The western part of the Deccan was then ruled by a king of the Yadava dynasty and Sarangadeva was a musician at his court. Situated as he was, geographically, Sarangadeva could see what was happening in south India as well as observe events in the north. North India was ruled by Muslim kings and they had at their courts musicians from Persia, Turkey, Arabia and Afghanistan. The Deccan was still under Hindu rule as was the south. Soon, however, the Deccan and a part of the south was to come under Islamic rule. Sarangadeva's *Sangeet-ratnakara*, therefore, forms a bridge; but more than that, it can be called the first modern book on Indian music.

In the seven chapters of his book Sarangadeva considers *swaras, srutis, jatis, tanas, gramas, murchanas,* and musical instruments. He also gives a resumé of the theories of other authors such as Narada of the *Sangeet-makaranda*, Bhoja, and Someswara.

The *Sangeet-ratnakara* is the first work to discuss the *ragas* in detail and it lists 264 of them. It gives the appropriate *ragas* for the hours of the day and night as well as for particular seasons. It even outlines a system of notation.

While discussing the *srutis* Sarangadeva gives them the following names:

Tivra, Kumadvanti, Manda, Chandovati, for the note SA.
Dayavati, Ranjini, Raktika, for the note RE.
Rudri and Krodhi for the note GA.
Vajrika, Prasarini, Priti, Marjani, for the note MA.
Kshiti, Rakta, Sandipini, Alapini, for the note PA.
Madanti, Rohini, Ramya, for the note DHA.
Ugra and Kshobini for the note NI.

From the distribution of his *srutis* it is clear that the parent scale *Sadja-grama* had gained ground by this time and that the other parent scale of the Age of Bharata, *Madhyama-grama*, was falling out of favour. Indeed, by the end of the 17th century *Madhyama-grama* was no longer in use.

Sarangadeva's contemporary Parsvadeva, author of the *Sangeet-samayasara*, is also worthy of note even though his book is overshadowed by the *Sangeet-ratnakara*.

The Islamic influence was now very much in evidence. Amir Khusro, born in 1234, was the first great Muslim musicologist of India. Although born in the Etah district in north India his forbears were Turks, and he thus called himself a Hindu Turk. As a disciple of Hazrat Nizamuddin Aulia he developed a philosophy of life that was humane, tolerant and intrinsically simple. However, apart from being an erudite scholar, poet, and musician, he was a polished courtier who served successive kings at the imperial court in Delhi. Very many years before the European Renaissance, Amir Khusro fulfilled its ideal of the complete man.

Music was Amir Khusro's great passion. He studied Persian, Arabic and Indian music and was so impressed by Indian music that he wrote: "Indian music, the fire that burns heart and soul, is superior to the music of any other country". He went to the humblest Hindu teachers to learn at their feet and he was not afraid of innovation. He therefore introduced Persian and Arabic elements into Indian music thus giving to it an added grace and elegance.

During his long life — he lived till the age of ninety — Amir Khusro attained legendary fame and official historians of the time often credited him with much more than he had done. Many believe, for instance, that he was the inventor of the *sitar*. In fact, Amir Khusro himself does not use the word in any of his writings. Now, was this undue modesty on the part of the inventor? The truth seems to be that Amir Khusro modified and improved the existing *veena* or *been*. He changed the order of the strings and made the frets movable. His improved *veena* would have been much like the modern *sitar* which word comes from the Persian *'seh-tar'*, 'three-stringed'. Since Amir Khusro was a Persian scholar it is presumed that he must have named the new instrument. This is not so, as the word *sitar* does not appear until well after his time.

Similarly there is an apocryphal account of how in a spate of invention he cut the *pakhavaj* (a drum with twin striking surfaces) in half, thus creating the two small drums of the *tabla*.

Amir Khusro invented new *ragas* such as *Sarfarda* and *Zilaph*; he introduced the *Qawwali*, a form of Muslim religious singing in which many voices are used; and he was the originator of the *Tarana* style of vocal music. Till recently it was supposed that the *Tarana* style used meaningless syllables just for the sake of exciting entertainment — rather in the manner of jazz singers. It was, however, pointed out by Ustad

Amir Khan in 1964 that when the syllables were pieced together they formed recognizable Persian words that had a mystic symbolism.

Allauddin Khilji, Sultan of Delhi (1296-1316), was the most illustrious monarch to be served by Amir Khusro. It is believed that the Sultan persuaded Nayak Gopal, another great musician, to translate the ancient *Dhrupad* songs into a living spoken tongue. The *Dhrupads*, whose original name was *Dhruvapada*, were Sanskrit verses that were sung in an austere manner. Nayak Gopal, obviously a native of the Braj region that encompasses the areas of Mathura and Vrindaban to the south of Delhi, translated these songs into the language that he knew best, that is, Braj Bhasa. Tradition had it that the god Krishna also had been a native of Braj and so Nayak Gopal's choice of language received a kind of religious sanction. The result was that it soon became a convention for writers in north India to compose their religious and secular verses in Braj Bhasa. The Sanskrit domination on the culture of India was now all but over. This factor combined with the Islamic influence in the north to produce a peculiar effect on the development of music. In the north music tended to become freer, more creative and experimental; in the south it continued to retain its respect for the sanctity of the past.

After Amir Khusro's time the northern and southern styles became distinct; the former being called the Hindustani and the latter the Karnatic. Much has been written about the relative merits and demerits of the two styles and much of it is of an unpleasant, prejudiced nature. Today better counsels have prevailed, helped no doubt by easier travel and greater cultural intercourse. Karnatic musicians perform in the north and Hindustani musicians in the south; there exists an atmosphere of mutual respect and the northerners are willing to learn from the southerners and *vice versa*. It would be true to say that it has taken almost seven hundred years for the wheel to come full circle. The two styles have not merged into one — that would be undesirable and, indeed, disastrous — but they have never been nearer.

There is a contention that soon after the death of Amir Khusro, Indian music somehow went underground for a period of two centuries. There seems to be little foundation for this view after one has read the accounts of the Arab traveller Ibn Batuta. He visited the court of Sultan Mohammad bin Tughluq (1325-1351) and observes that the king had over two thousand musicians in his service. In fact, the Muslim rulers were well known for their patronage of the arts and especially of music. Ibrahim Shah Sharqi of Jaunpur (1401-1440) was responsible for the compilation of the Sanskrit treatise *Sangeet-siromani* which was dedicated to him and Zain-ul-Abidin of Kashmir (1416-1467) was famous for his love of music.

The poet-musician Vidyapati was born in 1395 and during the forty-five years of his life he advanced the cause of Hindu devotional music. Many of Vidyapati's songs, as well as those of Jayadeva, were appended to the *Raga-tarangini* of Locana-kavi. Also inserted into Locana-kavi's book were the names of *ragas* attributed to Amir Khusro. These additions by some mediaeval scholar or scribe has led to bitter controversies over the correct dates of Locana-kavi and the *Raga-tarangini*. In the meantime, Vidyapati's contemporary Kalinath, who served Raja Devaraya of Vijayanagar, was writing a massive and learned commentary on Sarangadeva's *Sangeet-ratnakara*. This commentary has proved to be of immense value to both scholars and musicians.

The second half of the fifteenth century saw musical endeavour moving in three different directions and we shall consider each separately.

Devotional music in the form of community hymn singing became immensely popular. The *Keertan*, sung prayer, was carried to the remotest villages by Sri Krishna Chaitanya, a saint who commanded respect throughout India. Chaitanya's influence was felt most especially in eastern India — Bihar, Orissa, Bengal and Assam. Up to this time, Hindu worship was a private matter between a man and his personal god; now, perhaps under Muslim influence, it began to take on a social aspect.

The *Dhrupads*, it will be remembered, were translated into Braj Bhasa during Allauddin Khilji's time. They now found a champion in Raja Man Singh Tomar of Gwalior (1486-1518). This ruler, who was himself an excellent musician, regularly called together his best artists and got them to formulate the rules and requirements of *Dhrupad* singing. The Raja's musical advisers, *nayakas*, numbered such well known figures as Bhanoo, Charju, Bakshu and Dhundhi. They compiled a book in Hindi entitled *Man Kutuhal* which enunciated the latest theories on music.

Musicians and performing artists of every sort flocked to Gwalior and, so great was Raja Man Singh Tomar's contribution to *Dhrupad*, that many began to believe that he was the originator of the form. Thus *Dhrupad*, revitalized and reformed, gained wide esteem.

Ironically, while *Dhrupad* was growing in stature, an anti-*Dhrupad* movement was under way in Jaunpur. The ruler here at the time was Hussain Shah Sharqi (1458-1528), who was also a good musician. For a long time many had felt that the *Dhrupad* style was too formal and austere and what Indian music required was a style that was less formal and more imaginative. So Hussain Shah Sharqi and his fellow musicians invented the *Khayal* style (from *khayal*, meaning imagination). The *Khayal* offered wide scope for technical brilliance, invention and imaginative treatment of secular and religious themes. There were, in the past, some indications that such a style was struggling to be born — as, for example, in Amir Khusro's *Qawwali* — but the final form only took shape with Hussain Shah Sharqi.

There was considerable rivalry between the *Dhrupadiyas*, the followers of the *Dhrupad* style, and the *Khayaliyas* who followed the new *Khayal* style. This rivalry was only resolved when, in the nineteenth century, the *Khayal* was more widely accepted.

At this point in history a Hindu-Muslim compact in the arts was being established. Sikandar Lodi, Sultan of Delhi (1489-1517), gave his blessing to the *Lahjat-é-Sikandar Shahi*, the first book on Indian music written in Persian and based on Sanskrit sources. Ibrahim Adil Shah II, Sultan of Bijapur in the Deccan (1580-1626) and a famous poet-musician of his day, composed songs in praise of Hindu deities and published them in his *Kitab-é-Nauras*. Hindus learnt from Muslim *ustads*, masters, and Muslims from Hindu *gurus*. Hindu princes employed Muslim musicians and Muslim princes Hindus.

The Bhagti movement, which was based on universal brotherhood, had much to do with this tolerant atmosphere. In Andhra Pradesh the Bhagvatulus, followers of Bhagti, started a type of religious dance-drama which came to be called *Kuchipudi*; and in Tamil Nadu the followers of Bhagti, known as Bhagvatars, started a similar type of dance-drama, the *Bhagvata Mela Nataka*. The first book to refer to these religious dance-dramas, which were essentially Hindu in inspiration and character, was the *Machupalli Kaifiat* of 1502 which was written under Muslim patronage. The Hebraic faiths, Judaism, Christianity and Islam have tended to frown on dance as a sacred art because of the phenomenon of temple prostitution, and yet in south India the Muslim princes welcomed Hindu religious dancers. In the latter half of the sixteenth century, terms from Muslim usage like *salamu* and *tillana* — both adaptations of Persian words — were added to *Dasi Attam*, one of the most sacred of the Hindu dance styles. In 1675, the Nawab of Golconda, Abdul Hassan Tahnisha, saw a performance of a *Kuchipudi* dance-drama. He was so impressed that he granted lands to the Brahmin dancers, with the stipulation that the tradition of the dance-dramas should be carried on. The land grants were inscribed on copper plate which, in south India, was symbolic of authority and perpetuity. This is an example of how a Hindu religious art was not only tolerated, but actually fostered by a Muslim ruler.

5 The Mughals

Temujin the Mongol (1162-1227), who adopted the name Genghis Khan, annexed parts of north India to his vast empire which stretched from the Black Sea to the Pacific. The Mongols had a genius for adopting the culture and religion of the peoples they conquered. From the Turkish Uigurs they took their laws and alphabet, and when Kublai Khan (1214-1294), the grandson of Genghis Khan, became emperor of China he made Buddhism the state religion and spread Chinese influence from the Arctic Ocean to Malaysia and from Korea to the borders of Hungary. Marco Polo, who served Kublai Khan for many years, was not unaware of the fact that the splendours of China, which he had seen and recorded, had been achieved under a foreign emperor.

In India, about 300 years later, similar splendours were observed under similar circumstances.

Timur (1336-1405) is known to history as Tamerlane (from Timur-é-Leng meaning "Timur the Lame"). He too was a Mongol conqueror who, after ravaging India in 1398, annihilated the Turks at Angora taking the emperor Bajazid I prisoner.

In fifth generation male descent from Timur was Babar (1483-1530). On his mother's side Babar was a descendant of Genghis Khan. He invaded India in 1526 and met the vast army of Ibrahim Lodi, the Afghan sultan of Delhi, on the plains of Panipat. By his superb leadership and valour Babar decisively won the day and became the emperor of India and the founder of the Mughal dynasty. The Mongols, or Mughals as they were known in India, had accepted Islam and Babar was a practising Muslim. He had, nevertheless, vanquished a fellow Muslim, Ibrahim Lodi, to start a new era in Indian history.

Babar is a fascinating figure; a poet, one of his first acts was to design and construct a water-garden in Delhi. He was a keen observer and his memoirs are filled with the most acute analyses of personal and state problems. He was, above all, a man of action; he is said to have swum the Ganges twice and ridden 160 miles on horseback in one period of forty-eight hours.

Such was the background and the ancestry of Jalal-ud-Din Mohammad (1542-1605), Akbar the Great, the grandson of Babar who was born at Amarkot while his parents were fleeing from their enemies. As a child he fell ill and was on the point of death when his father Humayun took an oath that should the boy recover he, Humayun, would willingly die in his stead. The prince did recover and within a short while his father passed away. So, at the age of fourteen, Akbar inherited a recently acquired empire that was threatened by enemies on all sides. He realized that his rule could last only if it acquired a moral basis, and this meant justice for the majority of his subjects, who were, of course, Hindus. He therefore concluded treaties with Hindu rulers, married a Hindu princess, appointed Hindu ministers and advisers and promoted Hindus to leading army commands.

There was complete religious freedom in Akbar's domains at a time when, for instance, in England Roman Catholics and Protestants were burning each other at the stake. At Fatehpur Sikri, his new capital a few miles from Agra, which he had built in a Hindu-Muslim style, Akbar entertained philosophers and divines of every known faith. He presided over philosophic and religious discussions and would often contribute views and comments that furthered tolerance and understanding. The new religion which he attempted to promulgate was an eclectic kind of deism.

The emperor's able minister and historian Abul-Fazl has set down meticulously all that he observed and heard at the time. The founding of Fatehpur Sikri itself was due to a miracle. Akbar, having no son, was always worried about the future of the dynasty. Then someone suggested that he visit a saint who

lived in a cave some distance from Agra. Akbar made the
pilgrimage to the holy man on foot and, within a short time
after this, the emperor's Hindu wife was with child. The boy,
Salim, became the emperor Jehangir. In gratitude Akbar built
a new city on the hill where the saint's cave was situated and on
the city's main gateway, said to be the tallest of its kind in the
world, the masons were ordered to inscribe a quotation from
the New Testament.

The arts flourished under Akbar. The orchestra which
played at the entrance to the palace was made up of sixty
musicians. "His Majesty," writes Abul-Fazl, "pays much
attention to music, and is the patron of all who practise this
enchanting art. There are numerous musicians at court;
Hindus, Iranis, Turanis, Kashmiris, both men and women.
The court musicians are arranged in seven divisions, each for
one day of the week." Abul-Fazl then lists the thirty-six
principal musicians. One of these was the famous Baz
Bahadur, poet, musician, and last Muslim king of Malwa,
whose love affair with the Hindu dancing girl Rupmati is
celebrated in folklore. However, the greatest musician at
Akbar's court was Miyan Tansen. "For a thousand years there
has not been a musician like Tansen," says Abul-Fazl. Indeed,
many Indians believe that Tansen was the greatest musician
that ever lived. So much legend has collected around Tansen's
name that it is difficult to dust off the fiction and lay bare the
facts about him.

His father, Makarand Pandey, was a Brahmin poet and
landowner who lived in a village called Baher near the city of
Gwalior. Makarand Pandey and his wife were childless for
many years and, in desperation, went to a Sufi *fakir* named
Mohammad Ghaus who blessed them saying that they would
have a son and that he would grow up to fame and fortune. A
boy was born to them in 1508 and was named Tanna. Later,
the *fakir* visited the Brahmin's home to see the child who had
come in fulfilment of his prophecy. Laying a hand on the boy's
head, he took some betel-nut that he was chewing and put it
into the child's mouth. Tanna was now the *fakir's* "son" and
was renamed Ata Mohammad Khan, thus becoming a
peculiar synthesis — a Brahmin Muslim. India, however,
knows Ata Mohammad Khan as Miyan Tansen or simply as

Tansen. "Miyan" means "husband", "master", or "Sir" — an
address expressive of respect. "Tansen" is made up of two
words: "taan", a succession of notes; and "sena", army. So
"Tansen" would mean roughly "he who commands an army of
notes". It is said that Akbar himself bestowed this title upon his
favourite musician.

From an early age Tansen displayed a talent for creating
sound. He was a remarkable ventriloquist and could imitate
birdsong. Often he would hide in his father's fields and roar
like a tiger so as to frighten animals or human trespassers. One
day a group of *sadhus* who had lost their way took a short cut
across a field of corn. Tansen roared from behind a bush and
the *sadhus* scattered unceremoniously in all directions.
Realizing that he had scared away holy men, Tansen showed
himself to them and said he was sorry. Greatly impressed by
the lad's character and vocal powers the *sadhus* suggested to
Makarand Pandey that he send his son to Swami Haridas, the
well known music teacher of Vrindaban. So, after due
consultation with the family astrologer, Tansen was sent to
Vrindaban. Tansen lived for a decade with his teacher and
Swami Haridas, an acknowledged master of the *Dhrupad* style,
taught him all he knew. Indeed, this ascetic scholar has the
distinction of having taught a large number of famous
musicians among whom were Baiju Bavra, Ramdas,
Manadali, Raja Sanmukhan Singh of Ajmer (who accompanied Tansen on the *veena*), and Rani Mrignaini of Gwalior who
was the wife of Raja Man Singh Tomar.

By the time Tansen had finished his training Raja Man
Singh Tomar had died but Mrignaini, now widowed but still
wielding much influence as the Dowager Rani, invited Tansen
to the court of Gwalior. It was here that the young musician
got his first experience of gracious living and etiquette. He
made a fine courtier, always remembering that he was first
and foremost an artist. From Gwalior Tansen went to Rewa
where Raja Ram Singh was his generous patron. All this time
the musician was becoming a mystic, a *yogi*. He composed
music, experimented with sound, and discovered the
potentiality of mental vibrations.

There are numerous stories about Tansen's powers as a
singer. It is said that when he sang the *raga Bahar* plants

would begin to flower. With *Megh Malhar* clouds would form and burst into rain; and with *Deepak* fires would start up and lamps be lit spontaneously.

When Akbar heard of Tansen's genius he lost no time in getting him to the imperial court where he was made one of the *Nava Ratna* or Nine Gems of the empire. This meant that the musician had been elevated to the highest possible level that any man, after the emperor himself, could attain. By virtue of being a member of this august body of men, Tansen had immense influence in political, diplomatic, religious, financial and judicial matters. The only other example of a professional musician rising to such heights was Paderewski who became Prime Minister and, later, President of Poland.

Even though he was a Muslim in name and in faith Tansen often visited Hindu temples to pray and to chant the Vedic verses. His output of *Dhrupads* was vast and many were written in praise of Hindu deities. To this day one branch of his descendants, known as the *Seniya gharana* (the school of Tansen), sing only the *Dhrupad* type of composition. He opened the way for other Muslim musicians to partake in, and create, Hindu religious music.

Some of the best known *ragas* performed today were composed by Tansen. The list includes *Miyañ-ki-Malhar*, *Miyañ-ki-Sarang*, *Miyañ-ki-Todi* and *Darbari*; the last written at the command of, and dedicated to, the emperor.

Musicologists remember Tansen as a codifier. During his time there were thousands of *ragas*, often overlapping, with a confusing plethora of names. He studied their characteristics, improved some, got rid of others, and finally made an acceptable list of about four hundred.

Tansen died in his eighty-second year and was buried at Gwalior next to the tomb of Mohammad Ghaus, the *fakir* who had foretold his birth. His small mausoleum is a place of pilgrimage, especially for musicians. There is a belief that singers who eat the leaves of the tamarind tree overshadowing Tansen's grave will receive a boon in the form of sweeter and more melodious voices. Many singers still go to Gwalior for the express purpose of chewing the leaves from Tansen's tree.

The poet Sripathi, a contemporary of Tansen, has written that while Akbar was the lord of mere men, Tansen was the lord of music. That is why the emperor called him *Sangeet Samrat*, Monarch of Music.

Tansen and his wife Hussaini had five children, four sons and a daughter. They all had Hindu as well as Muslim names. Saraswati, the daughter, became a leading player of the *veena*, which was her father's favourite instrument. Akbar arranged her marriage to a prince named Misri Singh, a *veena* player and pupil of Swami Haridas. Misri Singh is also known as Naubat Khan. In north India the *veena* is often called the *been*, and so the descendants of Saraswati and Misri Singh have over the generations been called *Beenkars*, that is, specialists of the *been*. Tansen's sons — Suratsen, Saratsen, Tarangsen and Bilas Khan — concentrated on the *rabab*, a stringed instrument invented by their father and different from the *rabab* of Persia or Afghanistan. The descendants of the four sons of Tansen were called *Rababiyas* which means that the *rabab* was their chosen instrument.

Swami Haridas, Tansen's guru, was born some time during the latter half of the fifteenth century and it is thought that his parents were Brahmins from Multan. The boy had the usual education reserved for members of the priestly caste but in his early youth he renounced the world and became a *sanyasi*, an ascetic. For most of his life he lived in Vrindaban, on the banks of the Yamuna, and devoted himself to yoga and music. Under the influence of the teachings of Nimbarka, the thirteenth century philosopher from Andhra, Swami Haridas became immersed in *bheda-bheda*, the doctrine which identified the individual with the Supreme Being. This led him to the symbolism of the Radha-Krishna myth where Radha represented the individual and Krishna the Supreme Being. To express this difference-cum-identity he turned to music for it was in the magic of music, he believed, that differences were dissolved. In this belief he composed many *Dhrupads* and so well known did they become that students flocked to Vrindaban from distant parts hoping to learn at the feet of Swami Haridas.

The reigns of Akbar's son Jehangir (1605-1627) and grandson Shahjehan (1628-1658) were, in many ways, even more artistically productive. Jehangir was a painter and a renowned patron of the arts and Bilas Khan became his chief musician. Shahjehan built the Taj Mahal, regarded as the greatest example of Indo-Islamic architecture, and his chief musician was Lal Khan, a celebrated singer and son-in-law of Bilas Khan. There was peace and prosperity in the subcontinent and the economy was healthy and stable.

Unfortunately a dynastic feud commenced when Shahjehan fell seriously ill in 1657. The emperor's third son, Aurangzeb, came out on top after he had had his three brothers put to death and his father imprisoned in the Agra fort.

Aurangzeb, a puritan in his personal life, was imperious and headstrong. Even so, he has been much maligned. It has been said, for instance, that he was anti-Art. He was no more anti-Art than Cromwell who had Milton, the poet and organist, by his side for years. Aurangzeb was, in fact, fond of music but he had convinced himself that rulers ought to suppress their natural inclinations and devote themselves to duties of state. He did, nevertheless, maintain musicians and dancers for the entertainment of his wives and daughters. Niccolao Manucci, an Italian adventurer who lived in India during Aurangzeb's reign, has written about the many performing artists at the Mughal court and notes that they were given names like "Ruby" and "Gazelle-eyed". However, since the emperor had withdrawn his personal patronage the best artists left the imperial court to seek employment in the provincial centres.

During the fifty years of his reign, Aurangzeb was particularly harsh towards his Hindu subjects and succeeded in destroying much of the goodwill that had been carefully nurtured between Hindus and Muslims up to that time. The Mahrattas rose against the Mughals, there were rebellions elsewhere, and soon the empire was being threatened from all sides. Aurangzeb's life is that of a man who would not bend and so was broken.

The two emperors who succeeded Aurangzeb, Bahadur Shah I and Mohammad Shah, were very unlike him. The latter's reign which lasted till the middle of the eighteenth century, was especially glorious for music because at his court were Sadarang and Adarang who brought the *Khayal* style to its fullest perfection. Sadarang wrote thousands of compositions and it is chiefly through his efforts that *Khayal* gained a level of popular respectability. Also at this time, according to S.M. Tagore, the *Tappa* style of music was refined and introduced into the classical repertoire by Miyań Shori of the Punjab. *Tappas* were songs composed and sung by Punjabi Muslim camel drivers and Miyań Shori, seeing that these songs had strength and feeling, made them acceptable to sophisticated audiences.

In general parlance Mohammad Shah is always referred to as Mohammad Shah *Rangila*; the word *rangila* meaning a man who is given to artistic pleasures. When Nadir Shah, the Persian conqueror, was advancing on Delhi in 1737 the emperor was watching a musical drama and no one dared interrupt his enjoyment of it. The producer, therefore, did some quick improvisation. He forced one of the performers, who was doing a comic part, to sing the news on the stage as part of the play. This incident was rather like that which occurred with an earlier Merry Monarch in England, when the Dutch were sailing up the Thames and Charles II was difficult to find since he was occupied with a lady friend. Mohammad Shah, of course, paid heavily for his dereliction of duty. Nadir Shah entered the city and put thousands to the sword.

The Mughal empire, as an effective political entity, could be said to have lasted for something like two centuries: from about the 1530s to the 1730s. Certainly there was an emperor in Delhi right up to the middle of the last century, but he was an emperor in name only. Indeed, the later Mughals present an interesting psychological phenomenon. They liked to believe that they were still the emperors of India but in fact had become kings of Delhi and the British, with their dynamic leadership and talent for organisation, were the paramount power in the subcontinent. The Mughals, in these circumstances, fought shy of asserting their authority lest it be proved to the world — and to themselves — that they had little or no means of exercising that authority. They seem, therefore, to have retreated from political affairs and responsibilities in the hope that something fortuitous would turn up in their favour. Much of their time was spent in artistic endeavour, quite clearly as a form of spiritual and emotional compensation for the loss of empire. Their courts were crowded with poets, painters, musicians and dancers of all kinds. Many of the later

Mughal rulers were themselves poets and composers of the first rank. The last of them, Bahadur Shah II who wrote under the pen name *Zafar*, was a famous poet, musician and composer. He wrote numerous *Ghazals*, poems set to music, and *Thumris*, romantic lyrics, which became immensely popular and remain so today. Bahadur Shah is also remembered as the patron and friend of the poets Naseer, Zouq, and the great Ghalib.

In 1857 there was an armed uprising against the British in India. This mismanaged though bloody affair was mercilessly put down and, in the end, the sorry episode was discreditable to both India and Britain. The British government decided that India was too much for the East India Company to administer and so the Crown took over the Indian territories and Victoria was proclaimed Empress of India. This meant that the moment of truth had arrived for Bahadur Shah *Zafar*, the sensitive poet and Hamletian figure of Indian history, for it was he who held the title, albeit meaningless, of Emperor of India. He was forthwith taken into custody and exiled to Burma where he died in 1862.

This was the official end of the Mughal empire with *Zafar* lamenting his tragedy in memorable poetry.

6   Musical Development

Large areas of southern India have been ruled by Muslim monarchs: Malik Kafur marched up to Madurai, the Mughal empire stretched right down to the river Kaveri and, at the end of the eighteenth century, the powerful Tippu Sultan ruled Mysore. Why then was the Islamic influence in south India so little, if ever, felt? The simple answer seems to be that south Indian society has always been very tightly knit and caste conscious. The dynasty or the political system might change but these had little effect on the way of life, the religion, or the art of the people. In recent years a Communist government has ruled in Kerala, one of the southern states. Many radical measures were introduced by this government but in the end religion and caste won the day; in short, the culture of the people of Kerala has remained unchanged.

Music, in south India, has been firmly rooted in the temple and the *alvars*, composers of hymns, have always had an important part in it. Among the earliest *alvars* were Jnanasambandha in the seventh century and Periyalvar in the ninth. Their tradition of music reached a high point with Purandaradasa who lived at the same time as Tansen. Purandaradasa was a Vaishnavite, a devotee of the god Vishnu, and his many hymns are popular to this day. The musicologist Ramamatya, a contemporary of Purandaradasa, proved in his *Swaramelakalanidhi* that Karnatic music — the classical music of south India — was untouched by Muslim influence. Ramamatya, a descendant of Kalinath who a century earlier had written the well known commentary on the *Sangeet-ratnakara*, was a minister at the Vijayanagar court and it is obvious that when he spoke of music he included the music which was performed there. So we see that, as late as the mid-sixteenth century, even the secular music of south India was untouched by outside influence.

The arts flourished in the Vijayanagar empire and it was a period of great splendour and extravagance. Music and dance had reached a high level of excellence. The Muslim rulers to the north of the powerful Hindu empire were under constant threat from it and an important cause of friction was the disputed territory of the Raichur *doab*. *Ab* is the Persian word for water and, by extension, river and *do* is two; *doab*, therefore, means the land lying between two rivers. The Raichur *doab* is the rich triangular area between the rivers Krishna and Tungabhadra. The main city of this region is, of course, Raichur. For years there were protracted negotiations and recriminations over the ownership of the territory. Finally, the sultans of the Deccan decided to resolve their differences and, forming a confederacy, declared war on Vijayanagar. In 1565 the opposing forces met at Talikota in the Raichur *doab*. The Vijayanagar army was defeated with the result that a large part of the empire was taken over by the Sultan of Bijapur.

Fortunately this change in rulers, from Hindu to Muslim, made no difference to the development of music and dance. The Deccan sultans were themselves generous in their patronage of the arts and they invited Hindu musicians and dancers to their courts. *Dasi Attam*, the classical temple dance of south India now known as *Bharata Natyam*, was popular at the Muslim courts and it was at this time that terms adapted from Persian words began to be used in *Dasi Attam*. In music the south Indian musicians seem to have accepted some of the north Indian *raga* names as is evident from Somnatha's *Ragavibodha*, (1609).

Reference has already been made to Ibrahim Adil Shah II of Bijapur and his *Kitab-é-Nauras* in an earlier chapter, and he is not an isolated example of Hindu-Muslim understanding and amity. Indeed, among the aristocracy of Bijapur and Golconda it was not uncommon for Muslims to marry Hindu wives and for Hindus to marry Muslim wives. This pattern was followed by the musicians and the result was reflected in the music.

The time had now arrived for the proper codification of Karnatic music and the moment found the man in Venkatamakhi, the greatest musicologist of south India. His *Chaturdandi-prakashika* (1660) regrouped all the *ragas* under seventy-two parent scales or *melakartas* and his system is still followed by the musicians of south India.

Earlier, in north India, a similar attempt at musical reorganisation was made by Tansen. At the same time Raja Burhankhan, the ruler of Khandesh, which was north of present day Bombay, was the moving spirit behind another such attempt. Burhankhan commissioned Pundarika Vitthala for this work and the scholar produced his *Sadraga-chandrodaya* by the closing years of the sixteenth century. Another book, *Sangeet-darpana*, on the same lines was written by Damodara Misra in 1625.

Surprisingly, there was a spate of writing on musical subjects during Aurangzeb's reign as emperor of India. Hridaya Narayana wrote his *Hridaya-kautaka* and *Hridaya-prakasa*; Ahobala wrote *Sangeet-parijata* which was later translated into Persian by Pandit Dinanath; Fakir Allah wrote *Rag-darpan* in Persian and translated *Man Kutuhal*, the compilation of Raja Man Singh Tomar's time, into Persian; and Bhava Bhatta, who was at the court of Raja Anup Sinha, wrote three books on musical theory.

Seeing that Karnatic and Hindustani music were drifting apart in certain technical respects these north Indian writers made a conscious effort to establish a link. So we notice that they too, like Venkatamakhi, listed the *ragas* under their *melakartas* or parent scales. This was a departure from the *murchana*, modal, classification that Sarangadeva followed in his immensely influential *Sangeet-ratnakara*.

By the end of the seventeenth century, the classical music of both northern and southern India had arrived at a point of stabilisation. This stabilisation was seen at its best in the next century when Vishnupur, in eastern India, became a centre of musical activity of all kinds. Bahadur Khan, a descendant of Tansen, settled there and led a school of *Dhrupad* artists who, under the patronage of Raja Raghunath Singha, gained wide fame.

In the meantime, due to the impact of Venkatamakhi, the

music of south India had made tremendous progress. It was waiting for a golden age and this came with the birth of Thyagaraja in 1760. Born of Telugu speaking Brahmin parents at Thiruvarur in the Tanjore district, Thyagaraja displayed rare musical talents from a very early age. The family were cultured but of modest means although not without connections, for the boy's grandfather Giriraja had served in the Tanjore palace as the ruler's favourite poet. Consequently, he was sent for his education to the eminent Venkatramanayya under whom he studied Sanskrit, Telugu, Tamil, yoga and music. When Thyagaraja was fourteen his father died, and he had to abandon his studies and return home. Within a year his saintly mother Shantamma died as well and these two tragic events, so soon following one upon the other, appear to have transformed the boy's attitude to life.

His father had bequeathed to him a golden image of the god Rama and the orphan boy took to praying before the idol with great passion and feeling; he poured out his innermost thoughts to the god and discovered, as it were, a focus for his deepest emotions. He would spend days composing hymns to Rama oblivious of what was happening in the world around him. His elder brother Japyesa, believing that he ought to be doing something useful and earning a respectable living, had the image stolen hoping thereby to remove the cause of his brother's distraction from gainful employment. Instead, the loss of the image only sharpened Thyagaraja's anguish. He became even more introverted and composed with greater fervour. While singing he is said to have often experienced mystical ecstasies and *darshans*, divine visitations. Perhaps St. Teresa of Avila or the Sufi mystics might have understood this Hindu saint better than his own family. Indeed Roberto di Nobili, the famous Jesuit priest who lived at Madurai during that period, had the greatest respect for Thyagaraja.

Thyagaraja's two thousand or more *kritis*, religious songs, are a wonderful combination of music and words. He used his native tongue, Telugu, and wrote simple poetic prose. He then set his prose poems to *sangathis*, musical phrases, taken from a variety of *ragas*. This was an innovation and started a healthy movement against the heavy, stilted verse that Karnatic composers had come to accept as musical material. His *Pancharatnas* were made up of five *raga* patterns and his monumental *Shataraga-ratnamalika* used as many as a hundred. In a number of his hymns Thyagaraja used folk melodies and verses from folk-song, and thus became the preserver of folk art also.

Thyagaraja's great reputation as a saint-musician has eclipsed his achievements in secular music. It is, for instance, forgotten that he wrote three operas which were well known during his lifetime. He is, in fact, the father of modern Telugu opera. However, it is as a composer of religious music in the wider sense and not in the sense of music meant for temple ritual, that Thyagaraja is remembered in India. Many believe that he was a reincarnation of Valmiki, the sage of ancient India, who wrote the *Ramayana* as an epic poem of twenty-four thousand verses. His musical disciples reverently refer to his songs as *Thyag-upanishads*, for to them they have the sanctity of holy writ.

Thyagaraja's many pupils later formed three distinct schools of music and among his devoted followers were Venkataramana Bhagvatar, Krishna Bhagvatar, Manambuchavadi Venkata-subbayar, the Umalayapuram brothers, and Chakravarti Vina Kuppaiyar who became the master's most famous disciple.

In two of his songs Thyagaraja said that his *ishta-deva*, guardian deity, had promised him *moksha*, liberation of the soul, after he had completed his sojourn on earth, and in his philosophical speculations he stated that a knowledge and appreciation of music was a prerequisite for the attainment of *moksha*. He made a prophecy about his death and he passed away peacefully in his eighty-eighth year on the day and at the hour that he had foretold. His *samadhi*, shrine, is at Thiruvaiyar where an annual festival is held to celebrate the saint's life and musical achievements. No concert or recital in south India is regarded as complete without the inclusion in the programme of at least one of Thyagaraja's compositions.

Thyagaraja's two great contemporaries, Mutthuswamy Dikshitar (1775-1835) and Shyama Sastri (1763-1827), were also born at Thiruvarur. They are known as the *Trimurti*, or Trinity, of Karnatic music. Even though Dikshitar and Sastri wrote mostly in Sanskrit their music has many similarities to that of Thyagaraja.

The other composer of note, and one who has been somewhat overshadowed by the musical *Trimurti*, was Swati Tirunal (1813-47) who made a remarkable contribution to Karnatic music during his comparatively short life.

We must now turn our attention to other developments in India's cultural history.

London-based *sarod* player *Gurdev Singh* is a pupil of *Amjad Ali Khan*. *Photo: Avinash Pasricha.*

Amjad Ali Khan, the celebrated *sarod* maestro, who is the first north Indian musician to have played at Thyagaraja's shrine. *Photo: Y. Sahota*

7   The British

When the British first came to India as traders many of them adopted the way of life and the fashions of the Indian upper classes and took Indian wives. The Company Style of painting, which took its name from the East India Company, became popular; music and dance were often patronised by the rich merchants; and some even wrote verse of a good standard in the Urdu language. There is a theory that the British male was well on his way to being assimilated into the life of the sub-continent when, with the introduction of steamships and easier travel to India, the British woman arrived on the scene and soon put an end to British men 'going native'. This theory has some validity for the *memsahib*, the British woman in India, has always played a dominating and governess type rôle in her relationships with her own family and with Indians at large.

The British merchants had by the middle of the eighteenth century become the economic rulers of India. With Clive's victory at Plassey in 1757 these merchants also became the effective political rulers. Vast fortunes were amassed and economic historians recognize that the exploitation of India certainly helped Britain's industrial growth and eventual mercantile pre-eminence. Every Briton in India, however, was not of the exploiting class and the greatest of these scholar-administrators was Sir William Jones (1746-94). After a brilliant academic career at Harrow and University College, Oxford, Jones was called to the bar and secured a judicial post in London. At the same time he published a Persian grammar, a translation of Arabic poems, and a book about Latin commentaries on the poetry of Asia. He then went to Calcutta as a judge and immersed himself in the study of Sanskrit. Jones was the first Orientalist to write about the resemblance between Sanskrit, Greek and Latin. He translated *Shakuntala*, a play by Kalidasa the best known dramatist of ancient India, the writings of Manu and some portions of the *Vedas*. In 1784 Jones founded the Asiatic Society of Bengal which has since done tremendous work in the field of cultural studies.

Jones, a master of thirteen languages, was first attracted to Hindu drama and this led him to make a thorough study of Indian music. His famous treatise, *On the Musical Modes of the Hindus* (1784), begins with the following words: "Musick belongs, as a Science, to an interesting part of natural philosophy, which by mathematical deductions from constant phenomena, explains the causes and properties of sound, limits the number of mixed, or harmonick, sounds to a certain series, which perpetually recurs, and fixes the ratio, which they bear to each other, or to one leading term; but, considered as an Art, it combines the sounds, which philosophy distinguishes in such a manner as to gratify our ears, or affect our imaginations, or, by uniting both objects, to captivate the fancy while it pleases the sense, and speaking, as it were, the language of beautiful nature, to raise correspondent ideas and emotions in the mind of the hearer; it then, and then only becomes what we call a fine art ...." The erudition, the lucidity and the beauty of his English prose make this a work of genius. Not only does Jones describe Hindu music but he refers to Chinese, Greek, Persian and European classical music as well.

A practical study of Indian music was later made by Captain N. Augustus Willard who was a fine player of a number of Indian instruments. He was employed by the Nawab of Banda and spent much of his time studying with the musicians at the ruler's court. In 1834 Willard published *A Treatise on the Music of Hindustan* in which he gives an accurate picture of the state of music during his time. In short, his work was in the nature of a contemporary survey. Willard, in fact, criticises Jones and his followers for being too academic and out of touch with what Indian musicians were actually performing. He was one of the first to realize that by the beginning of the nineteenth century there was a division in north Indian music between its theory and its practice. This was a perceptive observation and one to which we shall return later.

The persuasive pen of William Jones has attracted many scholars from the West to a wide variety of Indian subjects. Among those who concerned themselves with music were: Bird, Fowke, Gladwin, Wilson, Ouseley, Tod, Campbell, Wood, Blochmann, Bosanquet, Chrysander, Engel, Burnell, Day, Hall, French, Grosset, Heymann, Regnaud, Hunter, and Lévi. In our own century the number of foreign writers, musicians, composers and musicologists who have studied Indian music is quite large. It would be impossible to detail here the contribution of each; suffice it to say that the work of some of them has been absolutely vital, and reference to them will be made as and when it is relevant.

There can be no justification for one nation ruling another, but history has strange lessons to teach. Consider the case of the cultural renaissance in India which found its highest expression in the life and work of Rabindranath Tagore (1861-1941). This renaissance started and flowered in Bengal, the province from which the British first ruled the whole of their Indian empire and where they had the strongest political and commercial power. A few years before Tagore's birth the British established a university in Calcutta, the second city of the Empire. It was modelled on London University. The medium of instruction was English and soon the best families of Bengal were sending their sons to be educated in Calcutta under British professors. This resulted in the formation of a Bengali intellectual class which, finding inspiration in the works of Shakespeare, Scott and Shelley, started literary experiments in their own language. Thus was born the modern Bengali theatre and the novel, and the poetry of Bengal received a fresh stimulus and direction.

The process of making Indians aware of their heritage was greatly furthered by the researches of Max Müller (1823-1900), a naturalised Briton of German descent, who was professor of comparative philology at Oxford. In 1847 the East India Company commissioned Müller to edit the *Rig-Veda*, the earliest of the sacred Hindu texts, and from then on his reputation soared in India and in the West. After Independence a cultural centre in New Delhi was dedicated to his memory and recently a special postage stamp honouring his name was issued in India.

Müller was not alone in this field. H.T. Colebrooke (1765-1837), aroused interest in India with his many essays and *Sanskrit Grammar*; H.H. Wilson (1786-1860), professor of Sanskrit at Oxford, helped to lay the foundations of Indian philology with his dictionary and grammar; John Muir (1810-82), author of *Original Sanskrit Texts* in five volumes and *Metrical Translations from Sanskrit Writers*, founded a chair of Sanskrit at Edinburgh; Monier Monier-Williams (1819-99), Sanskrit professor at Oxford, established the Indian Institute there; and William Wilson Hunter (1840-1900), a statistician who, as director-general, organised the 1872 census of India, wrote *A Comparative Dictionary of the Non-Aryan Languages of India* apart from other important works.

There were others as well and it is in the achievements of this dedicated group of men that one can find a real basis for East-West dialogue and understanding.

'Mandolin' Srinivas the popular musician from South India.
Photo: Om Subramaniam

Lalgudi Jayaraman whose artistry as a violinist is well known.
Photo: Om Subramaniam

8 The Modern Era

Whereas the south Indian musicians have resolutely adhered to the categories of Venkatamakhi, their north Indian counterparts found themselves, at the beginning of the nineteenth century, very far indeed from ancient usage. Creatively they had expanded to such an extent that theory had been left behind, sloughed off, or even ignored. There was, as Willard observed, a hiatus between what scholars thought music should be and what musicians were creating in the course of their daily duties. There were three reasons for this: firstly, the musicians — both Hindu and Muslim — were not educated enough to be familiar with ancient musical theory; secondly, since music was transmitted as a practical craft from father to son or from teacher to pupil, the influence of the father or the teacher was greater than that of past precepts; and thirdly, the theorists had failed to see the changes that were taking place and were, therefore, unable either to understand or to interpret them. If blame is to be apportioned then it is the theorists who must bear most of it. Music, especially Indian music, is dead the moment it stops growing and the composer-musician cannot wait for the musicologist who is tardy.

By the end of the eighteenth century a fundamental change had come about in the music of north India. Hitherto the *suddha*, pure or natural, scale had been the equivalent of the Western D mode; now the accepted *suddha* was the equivalent of the Western C mode. In Western terms the move was from the Dorian to the Ionian. The Maharaja of Jaipur, Pratab Singh Dev, now felt that the time had come for this innovation to receive the blessings of the *pandits* and the sanction of the theorists. He convened a conference for this purpose and published *Sangeet-sar* (1800) which formally recognized the change. Later, an aristocrat of Patna, Mohammad Rezza, brought out his *Naghmat-é-Asaphi* (1813). This book, written in Persian, made a considerable impression with its strong advocacy of the new *suddha* scale.

The next important writer was Kshetra Mohan Goswami whose *Sangeet-sara* (1863) continued the discussion on theory and practice. Goswami was encouraged by S.M. Tagore, himself an able musicologist, who published *Hindu Music from Various Authors* in 1882. Three years later Krishnadhan Banerji's *Gitasutra-sara* enlarged the understanding of Indian music to a great extent as the author had an excellent sense of

Subbulakshmi earned a great reputation as a vocalist. Her repertoire was drawn from both north and south India. Now in advanced years she is widely respected throughout India.

critical assessment. Banerji was well versed in Western music and was able to draw some interesting analogies. This awareness of Western music prompted Chinnaswami Mudaliyar to attempt the notation of Karnatic music and, in 1893, he published *Oriental Music in European Notation.*

The last decade of the nineteenth century saw, as we said in Chapter One, the publication of the original text of the *Natya Shastra* and this was followed a few years later by the discovery of a commentary on the book by Abhinava Gupta. These two events fortuitously coincided with the most fruitful years in the life of Vishnu Narayan Bhatkhande, without doubt the greatest Indian musicologist of modern times.

Born into a Maharashtrian family in 1860, Bhatkhande was trained in vocal and instrumental music by such well known teachers as V. Damulji, Raoji Belbagkar, Ali Hussain Khan, G. Jairajgir, and Vilayat Hussain Khan. He joined a music society in Bombay and there came into close contact with all kinds of musicians. While continuing his deep involvement with music, Bhatkhande qualified as a lawyer and made himself proficient in a number of Indian languages as well as English. For about fifteen years Bhatkhande studied every book on music that he could lay his hands on; if there were manuscripts in obscure languages or dialects that he did not know, he hired interpreters to translate them for him. All the time he would be taking notes, appending comments, making critical remarks, or busily adding on a word here or deleting a phrase there. Bhatkhande was essentially a scientist with an obsession for truth, clear thinking and lucid expression. He had little time for sages or musicologists, no matter how ancient or revered, who did not get down to brass tacks. In this respect Bhatkhande was very unlike his countrymen, for to most Indians a theory or idea is acceptable by the mere fact of its antiquity.

Bhatkhande soon discovered that a bewildering plethora of theories and practices had proliferated all over the country. Each *gharana*, school, had developed its own conventions and these, sanctified by time, were adhered to with fanatical faith. The first task he had to undertake, therefore, was to ascertain the facts about each *gharana*. Now this was no easy task as the *gurus* and *ustads* of the *gharanas* were never willing to discuss the workings of their craft guilds with an outsider. Bhatkhande, nevertheless, made numerous tours all over India and managed to persuade a number of *gharana* heads to co-operate with him. He visited every musical centre in the subcontinent, had discussions with teachers and musicologists, listened to the music of each *gharana*, spent weeks inspecting manuscripts in private hands, studied teaching techniques and wrote down rare songs. The opposition on the part of certain *gharanas* slowly melted away when they saw that he was an objective observer, completely impartial and not, in any way, likely to rob them of their livelihood. When, for instance, the phonograph first came to India it was very difficult to get any artist of standing to make recordings, since musicians had the feeling that if their work were recorded and sold, fewer people would attend their recitals. Also, there was a superstition that to permit your music to be recorded and taken away was tantamount to losing part of your being. The fact that Bhatkhande was a high-born and learned Brahmin was an advantage to him when facing this particular problem as with many other similar ones. He argued and cajoled and it was difficult to refute his authority. In the end Bhatkhande preserved many unusual and difficult *ragas*; in Jaipur, for example, he recorded more than three hundred songs by Mohammad Ali Khan and his sons Ashiq Ali and Ahmed Ali.

What fascinated Bhatkhande was the way in which different *gharanas* treated and rendered the same *raga*. Between 1920 and 1937 he published the results of his researches in six volumes of the *Kramik Pustak* series. After stating the interpretations of the performing artists, Bhatkhande gave his own comments and views. He also listed the musicians whose work he was considering, their place of residence and the *gharana* to which they belonged. Among these were three direct descendants of Tansen who were then at the Rampur court, namely, Mohammad Ali Basat Khan, Mohammad Vazir Khan and Mohammad Amir Khan. Later Raja Nawab Ali Khan of Lucknow, a follower and ardent admirer of Bhatkhande, continued with this study and brought out *Marif-ul-naghmat*, a book inspired by the *Kramik Pustak* series.

Of Bhatkhande's many other books and most important are

Lakshya-sangeet (1910), written in Sanskrit under the pseudonym "Chatur Pandit"; *Hindustani Sangeet Padhati* in four volumes, first written in Marathi and then translated into Hindi; and a collection of his own compositions titled *Lakshan-geetas* (1912). He also brought out editions of writers such as the south Indian Ramamatya and the north Indian Pundarika Vitthala.

Being of an ascetic and scholarly nature, Bhatkhande did not make friends easily. However, he had the type of personality that commanded respect without the use of many words. Many influential people such as the rulers of Baroda, Mysore, Rampur, Dharampur and Gwalior came under his spell and became crusaders for music. A number of music colleges were founded under Bhatkhande's guidance the most notable of which were the Madhav Music College at Gwalior, the Baroda State School of Music, the Faculties of Music at Benares Hindu University and the Poona Women's University, and the Bhatkhande Music College at Lucknow. The institute at Lucknow was headed by S.N. Ratanjankar, Bhatkhande's most devoted pupil.

Due to an attack of paralysis Bhatkhande was an invalid during his later years. He died in 1936, one of the most respected men in India.

Apart from Bhatkhande, there were a number of other people who worked ceaselessly for the cause of music. His fellow Maharashtrian, Vishnu Digambar Paluskar, established music colleges known as Gandharva Mahavidyalayas in many cities and this helped to make the profession of music acceptable to the middle classes. Sufi Inayat Khan of Baroda carried Indian music abroad by founding the Sufi Order of Universal Brotherhood in Europe and America; music and meditation forming an essential part of the order's disciplines. Rabindranath Tagore, who had founded his international university at Santiniketan in 1901, experimented with folk melodies and ensemble playing and created a new *genre* of music called *Rabindra-sangeet* which became immensely popular. There was also the indefatigable Atiya Begum Fyzee-Rahamin whose first book on Indian music appeared in 1913 and who lectured on the subject in many parts of the Western world. This lady, with the help of Bhatkhande and

Vinay Bharat-Ram was well known as a singer of the younger
generation. A Delhi industrialist, he is now an influential art
patron. The stringed instrument is a *tamboura*, or drone.

others, started a campaign for the holding of music
conferences at which musicians, teachers, musicologists and
critics from all over India could perform, hold dialogue and
make decisions.

In 1916 the Maharaja of Baroda convened the first All-India
Music Conference at Baroda. The objectives, some rather
idealistic, were set down in a draft memorandum. There were,
for example, lofty aims such as: "To effect if possible such a
happy fusion of the northern and southern systems of music as
would enrich both"; "To provide a uniform system of notation
for the whole country"; "To arrange new *raga* productions on

scientific and systematic lines"; and "To take steps to protect and uplift our Indian music on national lines". Among the more practical proposals were the following: "To collect in a great central library all available literature (ancient and modern) on the subject of Indian music and, if necessary, to publish it and render it available to our students of music"; "To start an *Indian Men of Music* series"; and "To conduct a monthly journal of music on up-to-date lines".

Very little of the above was actually achieved, but the conference did create an awareness in the minds of the general public of what had to be done for the preservation of an important part of their cultural heritage. For the musicians themselves the conference was interesting. Artists of widely differing styles and traditions got to know each other and became conversant with each other's techniques, and Bhatkhande presented a paper, *A Short Historical Survey of the Music of Upper India*, which has since become well known.

Nawab Hamid Ali, the ruler of Rampur and a friend of Bhatkhande, was the president of the second All-India Music Conference which was held at Delhi in 1918. The Nawab and his son Prince Sadat Ali were fine musicians and were pupils of Mohammad Vazir Khan and Mohammad Amir Khan, two of Tansen's descendants. In fact, Bhatkhande has studied the *raga* interpretations of the Nawab and his son in the *Kramik Pustak* series. At the conference the Nawab announced that he had opened his archives for scholarly research and that the sixteenth century *Dhrupads* in his possession were to be recorded for the phonograph. Two outstanding papers were read. Krishna Rao's *Emotion in Music* outlined the psychological implications of the musical experience and Ganpatrao Chavan, expanding on this subject, suggested research into the therapeutic value of music.

The emphasis seems to have been on *Dhrupad* music although Sadat Khan's playing on the *jaltarang*, the Indian equivalent of the glass harmonica, caused quite a sensation.

Some other Indian princes now interested themselves in music, the most influential among them being the rulers of Alwar, Nabha and Indore.

The third All-India Music Conference was held at Benares in 1919 with the Maharaja of Benares in the chair. The chief attraction of that year was the Baroda orchestra which was made up of Indian instruments. M. Fredilis, the head of the Baroda State School of Music, was the conductor and his commendable attempt to orchestrate Indian music was well received.

After this there was a gap of six years, and the fourth All-India Music Conference was convened at Lucknow in 1925. The Nawab of Rampur, who was to preside, could not attend on account of a bereavement and the chair was taken by Sir William Marris, the governor of the United Provinces. The moving spirit of the conference was Raja Nawab Ali Khan who made a powerful plea for Indian music to be taught in Indian schools.

In the meantime two scholarly civil servants, one Indian and the other British, started a study of intonation in Indian music. K.B. Deval published his theories in *The Hindu Musical Scale and the Twenty-two Srutees* (1910) and E. Clements, while setting down the results of their researches in *Introduction to the Study of Indian Music* (1913), strongly condemned the increasing use of the Western harmonium in India.

Clements came down very hard on those who wanted to use tempered instruments or were enamoured of Western staff notation. Deval inspired H. Keatley Moore to design a harmonium which, they claimed, was suitable for Indian music. This instrument was patented by Keatley Moore and did actually appear in the shops. Continental harmonium manufacturers, however, flooded the Indian market and the new instrument had a short commercial life.

Interest in the improvement of musical instruments was sustained by A.M. Meerwarth's *Guide to the Musical Instruments in the Indian Museum, Calcutta* (1917). This matter was, in fact, raised at the Lucknow music conference when it was suggested that there was a great need for a higher standard of instrument making.

The Music of Hindostan (1914) by A.H. Fox Strangways and *The Music of India* (1921) by H.A. Popley were two books that received well deserved commendation when they came out. These two books, now naturally dated, brought Indian music to the attention of a large number of people. Among the later musicologists whose work deserves particular mention are H.L. Roy, G.H. Ranade, Swami Prajnanananda, O.C. Gangoly, P. Sambamoorthy, Abdul Halim, Alain Daniélou, M.S. Ramachandran, O. Goswami, Peter Crossley-Holland, W. Kaufmann, A.A. Bake, A.N. Sanyal, H.S. Powers, Bishan Swarup, N.A. Jairazbhoy, Baburao Joshi, John Levy and Peggy Holroyde.

The partition of the subcontinent in 1947, and the emergence of two sovereign nations with the accompanying changes in the political and economic order, had far-reaching effects on cultural activity which will require detailed examination.

During Bhatkhande's time and after, the patronage of music and dance came largely from the princes and *zamindars*, feudal landlords. The Indian States were of varying sizes, from large ones like Hyderabad, Kashmir, Gwalior, Indore, Mysore and Patiala to the very small ones like those in the Simla hills. These princes always employed musicians at their courts and there was continual rivalry among them as to who could secure the services of a better singer or a more talented instrumentalist. That is why so many *gharanas* were either named after, or located at, the capital of a particular state.

The rest of the subcontinent was divided up into the various provinces of British India. It was in British India that the nucleus of a middle class began to take form. This was to be expected since it was in British India that education and industry first made their impact. Soon after independence the princes were brought to heel and their states incorporated into the new political structure. Having lost their power and much of their wealth, the princes could no longer afford to keep their musicians, whose future would have been extremely precarious had there not, in the meantime, been a veritable epidemic of cultural fever throughout the country.

Jawaharlal Nehru, the first prime minister of the new India, was a man of learning and was conscious of the fact that the country's heritage was a precious asset. His policy was one of encouragement to the arts at every level; a ministry of cultural affairs was set up under Humayun Kabir, an associate of Tagore; national and state academies of art, music and letters

were constituted; folk dance and youth festivals were organised
up and down the country. Nehru and his government were
often accused of placing too much emphasis on culture and too
little on agriculture. Whatever the justification for it, there is
no doubt that all this activity certainly helped the traditional
musicians. They were welcomed into the scores of newly
opened music departments in the universities and the
state-financed music colleges. All India Radio, the government controlled network under B.V. Keskar, the minister
responsible for broadcasting, embarked upon a massive
project of cultural uplift through classical music. Musicians
were summoned to Delhi from distant parts and honoured as
cultural heroes by the president of the republic. Through
radio and the record-player these artists found new audiences.
Their erstwhile patrons, the princes, might have gone under,
but the musicians of India were never better off.

Classical music had now become fashionable in India, at
least among the *nouveau riche* and the middle class that had
ousted the British. Although it must be said that in the south
and in Bengal the middle class interest in the arts had started
somewhat earlier, it was in the north, in what is called the
Hindi-speaking region, that the dramatic change came about
only after 1947 and, in the context of India, this is what is
significant.

Children, especially girls, were told that they must learn
music if they wished, in later life, to have any pretensions to
culture. In a largely arranged-marriage society the girl who
could sing or play an instrument after a fashion had a far beter
chance on the marriage market. Often crash courses were
arranged for a girl if it became known that the prospective
husband was keen on a *sitar* playing wife or that his family
would not even look at the girl if she were not musical.

The matrimonial columns in the respected national papers,
which are published in English, provide a good indication of
the part that music plays in the Indian marriage stakes. A
typical advertisement placed by a man or his family would
state how old the "boy" was (in these advertisements "man" is
seldom, if ever, used) and then give his caste or sub-caste, his
education, his profession, his salary and his family
connections; the requirement for this "boy" would be "a fair

complexioned virgin" of this or that caste or sub-caste, "convent educated" with "fluent English", and possessing "proficiency in music" or "a voice trained for singing".

With so much demand for musical training there is, inevitably, a shortage of good teachers. The cities of India are full of *gurus* and *master-jis* of doubtful qualification. Many of them run private colleges upon which they bestow high-sounding Sanskrit names. The instruction they impart is on a part-time basis and after a year or two of this they award certificates and diplomas, again with Sanskrit names. Since paper qualifications are highly regarded in India these spurious diplomas are not without their uses. The "graduates" of these colleges cannot become professional performers as they are just not good enough, so many of them either become "professors" at their old colleges or do even better and open their own colleges with equally high-sounding names. Bad teaching produces bad students who, in their turn, become teachers and produce more bad students; and so the chain continues. A number of such "trained musicians", however,

The *surbahar* is a bass *sitar*. Its leading player is *Imrat Khan* (left), younger brother of the famous *Vilayat Khan* (right) who plays the *sitar*. The portrait on the left is that of their father *Inayat Khan*, in the middle is their grandfather *Imdad Khan*, and on the right their uncle *Vahid Khan*.

are more ambitious and these join the film industry which provides them with a good living and a certain amount of glamour.

No discussion on music in India today can have any meaning without reference to the film industry. Films offer the only mass entertainment in India and the industry produces, on average, about 400 enormously lengthy films every year. In terms of footage this makes India one of the world's leading film producing countries. Every film must have background music together with a number of songs. It is these songs that form the staple musical diet of the vast majority of Indians. For years there has been heated controversy about what effect this facile orchestration, these plagiarised melodies from foreign sources, and the mixture of native and alien instruments would have on the musical sensibilities of the Indian people. Keskar, and others of his persuasion, believed that popular film music would not only deafen the ears to the subtleties of the microtones in Indian classical music but would also pollute the minds of the younger generation. Unfortunately, Keskar spoilt his own case by overplaying his hand. All India Radio adopted a puritanical line by broadcasting only classical music that was "morally pure". This step did more harm than good because people merely switched over to Radio Ceylon, a high-powered commercial station. In short, the government radio was brought into disrepute because it lost millions of listeners and a foreign-owned commercial radio profited from that loss. All India Radio's policy was later reversed and now "light" music is also broadcast.

On the whole, Indian film music has certainly had some very undesirable effects. Most of it is not so much Indian as a form of commercial hybridization from various sources. This orchestrated mush has been blaring away in thousands of villages for over a generation and has now started to influence the folk music of the peasants. This music springs from the very soul of the people and it would be a gigantic tragedy if the concoctions of the smart musicians in the Bombay studios were to injure so rich a folk tradition. Musicologists in India have paid little attention to this matter. This stems, quite obviously, from a mistaken notion that the Sanskrit or classical tradition is the Great Tradition and that regional and folk traditions constitute the Little Tradition. These terms are no more than labels; every tradition is worthy of respect, consideration, and careful conservation. Some useful work has been done with regard to folk dancing in India but very little indeed in the field of folk music.

When "graduates" of the private music colleges get into the sound studios they display a peculiar type of superiority and in an effort to show off their training they manage to inject what they think is classical music into films. The result is that millions of people hear a jazzed-up or mangled version of some sacred *raga* which they, in their innocence, believe is the real thing. This travesty is also perpetrated on classical dance; there was a time when the *Kathak* style of the north was abused in this way, now the southern *Bharata Natyam* style is the chief sufferer.

A few Indian films have, undoubtedly, been vehicles for some pleasing music but this has only been due to a handful of talented music directors such as Naushad Ali and S.D. Burman. The most famous voice in the country belongs to Lata Mangeshkar who has sung for more films than any other artist in the world, a fact that has earned her an entry in the Guiness Book of Records. Satyajit Ray is extremely careful in the choice of music for his films — he got, for instance, Ravi Shankar to do the music for the *Apu* trilogy and Vilayat Khan to do likewise for *Jalsaghar* — but, unfortunately, Ray's films do not get wide release in India. They are very much a minority interest.

The authentic teachers are, nevertheless, doing tremendously valuable work in the universities and *bona-fide* colleges. Their students are drawn from a wide cross-section of society thus making classical music more broad based. This is one of the praiseworthy changes that came about with independence. No more is music the monopoly of a particular caste, and many young men and women with the necessary talent now have the opportunity of being trained properly. Today a number of well known musicians and dancers come from middle class families which, in the past, had no connection with the arts. Indeed, not very long ago, many of these same families were positively against music and dance since these arts were thought of as the twin paths to hell and the saboteurs of respectability. India, however, is a long way from what, in the West, would be called equality. Caste, although abolished by law, is still a force to be reckoned with. The new recruits to music and dance come from middle class Hindu families of the three higher castes: it would be difficult to find a single classical musician or dancer who belongs to the Shudra caste, members of which were known as Untouchables and were later called *Harijans* ("God's beloveds") by Gandhi. This is something that people in the West will find extremely difficult, if not impossible, to comprehend. For example, the daughter of a lavatory attendant in Europe or America can dream of becoming, and even become, a concert pianist or ballet dancer. In India, a lavatory attendant would certainly be a Shudra and his daughter could never — in the present circumstances — aspire to becoming a professional artist in any field. This is a fact that educated people in India, who like to talk of democracy and egalitarianism, might not like: it is, nevertheless, one of the facts of Indian life. Things are changing, very slowly, and it is possible that in the dim, distant future the arts of India might, in truth, become the heritage of all Indians.

Broadly speaking, those who learn from *gurus* and *ustads* can be divided into two categories: *sishyas* or *shahgirds* and students. Hindu *gurus* call their disciples *sishyas* and Muslim *ustads* call theirs *shahgirds*. It is not easy to be accepted as a disciple by a reputable *guru* or *ustad* for these teachers are extremely careful in their selection. When a decision is made there is a solemn ceremony of initiation which inaugurates the *guru-sishya* or *ustad-shahgird* relationship. Such a relationship is not entered into lightly by either party for it is a life-long connection. Apart from the *sishyas* and *shahgirds* there are the music students who are to be found mainly in the university music departments. They are instructed by *gurus* and *ustads* whom they respect greatly even though the intimate *guru-sishya* relationship does not exist. The atmosphere is similar to that which prevails in the music academies of the West. The music graduates from the universities are the secularized concert hall artists of today who now form an entirely new class of musicians. So we see the old system and the new existing side by side which, in the world of music, signifies a healthy state of affairs. There can, however, be no doubt that within the next decade or so the new system will predominate. Because musical training is now more organized and widespread, a larger number of musicians are now on the market. For this reason alone some people believe that the quality of musicianship is suffering in favour of quantity. The facts do not bear this out; India has never had so many good musicians and competition has never been fiercer. It is only when there are a large number of good musicians about that there can be any hope for one or two great ones to emerge.

Admittedly, some cities do seem to have a lot of musical activity in the form of festivals of one kind or another. This should not worry anybody. Let the artist who feels he is worthy, appear on the platform. Time soon sorts out the excellent from the indifferent.

Independence ushered in better rail and air transport. This meant that musicians become mobile and could very easily have extended tours of the country. Karnatic musicians performed in the north and Hindustani musicians in the south. This has resulted in the exchange of musical ideas. Hindustani music is no longer thought of as *outré* in the south and the same can be said of Karnatic music in the north.

The Sangeet Natak Akademi, the national academy of music, dance, and drama, was founded in 1953. The other two academies are the Sahitya Akademi for letters, and the Lalit Kala Akademi, for art. Over the two decades of its existence the Sangeet Natak Akademi has promoted the cause of music with admirable fortitude. Funds have been lamentably low and there have been many charges of favouritism. However, in spite of its many ups and downs, the Sangeet Natak Akademi continues to perform a useful task.

Indians are, as a people, extremely impressed by position and power. Politicians, therefore, exploit this situation. They seek and are readily offered the presidentships of music societies, art groups and theatre and dance companies. One can recall, with a shudder, many musical evenings ruined by a half hour platitudinous introduction to aesthetics by a cabinet minister.

Apart from politicians and V.I.Ps., the audiences themselves need to be educated in the simple courtesies of

The *shehnai* is India's nearest equivalent to the oboe and its greatest living master is *Bismillah Khan* of Varanasi. His style has dominated *shehnai* playing for decades.

social behaviour. Often, in the middle of an intense solo, a lady bedecked like a christmas tree will clatter in her fashionable shoes down the aisle and claim her seat in the front row. She is obviously the wife of a minister or senior official. Someone near your left ear will then decide to start a conversation with his neighbour on the merits of a particular piece and no amount of glaring will have any effect. The ruination of the evening is finally completed when a babe in arms feels the pangs of hunger and starts exercising his little lungs. It might be a worthwhile idea for the Sangeet Natak Akademi to start a series of lectures on concert hall behaviour, especially in north India for that is where the need is greatest.

We must now look at music in those areas which not long ago were a part of India.

In 1947 a truncated India gained independence and, at the same time, Pakistan was born. Another country, Bangladesh, has since come into being. What was one country in 1947 is now three countries. Let us consider Pakistan first.

Within a short period it is difficult for any country to establish a cultural identity; especially when, as in Pakistan's case, there have been many internal and external problems. Pakistan's *raison d'etre* was more than just a political or religious one: it was a conscious effort to break away from the mainstream of Indian culture which was inextricably bound up with the theories and practices of the Vedic past and the Hindu present. This was unfortunate for the arts in Pakistan with the exception of poetry and literature generally, which flourished. The middle class and those who had amassed wealth during Pakistan's early years have little time for the arts. The cultural scene presents an unflattering picture and it is a problem which will, sooner or later, have to be considered very seriously by the country's leadership and intelligentsia. Pakistan will have to discover and understand her cultural past — pre-Aryan, Vedic, Greek, Arabic, Persian, Turkish, Hindu and indigenous Islamic — and only when that heritage has been firmly grasped can there be optimism for the future.

At the time of partition some Muslim musicians migrated to Pakistan; among the seniormost of these was Bundu Khan of Indore, the famous *sarangi* player, who died a few years ago. Nazakat Ali and Salamat Ali, the celebrated *Khayal* singers, were born in east Punjab in India. The terrible conditions of the civil unrest in 1947 forced these two brothers to flee their homes and go to Pakistan where, fortunately, they did well. Malika Pukhraj of Jammu also left India. She is a great singer of *Ghazals* and *Thumris* and has fanatical devotees in Pakistan and India. The popular singer Noorjehan was known as Bulbul-é-Hind (the Nightingale of India) before partition. When she went to Pakistan she became Bulbul-é Pakistan. Among the *qawals*, exponents of songs with Muslim themes, the most celebrated are Ghulam Farid Sabri, Nusrat Fateh Ali Khan, and Munshi Raziuddin Ahmed.

Like India, Pakistan is also flooded with commercial music and neither country has yet evolved a definite policy with regard to film music.

The coming into being of Bangladesh, formerly East Pakistan, discredited the theory that people with the same religion must necessarily have the same culture. The conflict between the two wings of Pakistan was largely a cultural one. The east Bengalis, for example, were incensed when Tagore's music, *Rabindra-sangeet*, and poetry were officially discouraged by the government on the grounds that Tagore, besides being a Hindu, was regarded as the national poet of India. The east Bengalis may have had negative feelings about Tagore on these two scores but they were far outweighed by their positive feelings that Tagore was a great *Bengali* poet-composer whose art was being suppressed by Punjabi-speaking or Urdu-speaking administrators. They believed, in short, that their heritage was being destroyed by their compatriots from the western wing. There was no cultural bond between the two wings and it was only a question of time before the two parts of Pakistan drifted away from each other.

Many of India's leading musicians come from Bangladesh and the country is particularly rich in folk music. From its very inception the new state has been beset with calamities. Only in the future will it be possible to give an accurate account of musical activity in Bangladesh.

Indian music in Europe and America presents a fascinating picture and deserves a separate discussion.

9 Indian Music and the West

We have already seen how, in the past, some of the leading minds of the West were attracted to India's culture and music. Later, musicians and composers also began to take a keen interest. *Quatre Poèmes Hindous*, by Ravel's pupil Delage, showed how Europeans could catch the mood of Indian music. Holst, greatly interested in Indian philosophy, composed many pieces on Hindu subjects; the best known of these being *Savitri*, a one-act opera. Debussy and Scriabin discussed music with Sufi Inayat Khan, were enraptured by his *veena* playing, and thenceforth held Indian music in the highest regard. Scriabin, in fact, invented a "mystic chord" of ascending fourths as he felt that the ordinary major and minor chords were inadequate to express his theosophical beliefs.

Sufi Inayat Khan was the first to take Indian music to the West. His recital at the Hindu temple at San Francisco on April 9, 1911, was the beginning of a tour that took him to many countries. Eventually he made his headquarters at Geneva with a branch at Suresnes, near Paris. His son, Hidayat Khan, who now lives in Munich, is a composer of western orchestral music and his magnum opus is the *Gandhi Symphony* written to commemorate the centenary of the leader's birth. Noor-un-nisa, Sufi Inayat Khan's eldest child, was a talented writer, composer and musician. During the last war she joined the W.A.A.F. and was landed in France to help the French Resistance. Under the code name "Madeleine" she performed some remarkably heroic deeds before she was betrayed to the Gestapo and sent to Dachau. There for nine months she was interrogated and tortured but did not break.

In anger and desperation the Nazis executed her by firing
squad. The British awarded her the George Cross, the French
the Croix de Guerre with Gold Star.

Choreographers and balletmasters have always been
interested in dances and themes from India. Taglioni did *Le
Dieu et La Bayadère*, Coralli *La Peri*, and Perrot *Lalla Rookh*.
Ruth St. Denis performed her *Radha* dance all over the world;
Diaghilev commissioned Fokine and Cocteau to create *Le Dieu
Bleu* in which Nijinsky and Karsavina danced the leading rôles
and Bakst was responsible for the scenery and costumes; the
great Pavlova herself travelled to India in search of
inspiration; at Covent Garden she danced *Ajanta Frescoes*,
based on the famous cave paintings, and her *Radha Krishna
Duet* with Uday Shankar became well known during its time.

Between the two world wars Uday Shankar toured Europe
and America with his dancers and musicians. The musicians in
his company included his younger brother Ravi, Vishnudas
Shirali, Timir Baran, and Ustad Allauddin Khan. Shankar's
company made a tremendous impression whenever they
appeared in Paris, London, or New York. It was during that
time that Yehudi Menuhin's interest in India began and today
he is the great champion of Indian culture in the West. Indeed
Menuhin and the Earl of Harewood have worked unceasingly
for the propagation of Indian music abroad. Harewood took a
particularly momentous step when, as director, he invited
Indian musicians to the Edinburgh Festival. From then on
Indian artists have been welcomed everywhere.

The Indian government has pursued a policy of sending
cultural delegations to various countries and this has greatly
facilitated international understanding. The authorities in
Delhi have generally been wise in the selection of their artists
and a considerable amount of vetting takes place before a
musician is sent abroad. There has, nevertheless, been an
unfortunate and dangerous development during the last few
years. Many "impresarios" and "cultural organizations", eager
to cash in on the popularity of Indian music and dance, have
started presenting inferior artists to audiences in the West.
Many musicians who find it difficult to make a career in
Indian now manage, by various means, to come abroad and
make a splash. Their most enthusiastic fans tend to be

European or American youths who are drop-outs from their own societies and who think that an attachment to anything Eastern confers a certain status.

Every month somewhere in the West an Indian musician or dancer appears on the scene. It has become quite a profitable industry. If the musician or dancer happens to be a dusky beauty so much the better; she very quickly collects admirers, "impresarios", and "managers". Third rate musicians and dancers are therefore written about and considered quite seriously. The glowing reviews, penned by uninformed and over-impressed Western critics, are then circulated in India. Not surprisingly, since the colonial mentality lingers on in India, these reviews and comments send up the artist's stock back home; and so by a circuitous and dubious route the artist "arrives" not only in the West but also in India. Colonialism has a lot to answer for: it has corrupted both the colonised and the coloniser.

The cultural organizers, most of whom are Indians, float non-profit making companies and charities and this gives them tax advantages. They then draw their "legitimate" expenses and salaries out of organization funds. Quite naturally people think that no one is making a profit whereas, in fact, the cultural organizers do extremely well out of it. They are essentially public relations men who are able to convince governments, the liberal press and the public that they are doing a marvellous job in the field of international amity through the medium of the arts. Airlines, eager to stimulate tourism, provide the organizers and the artists they get from India with free transport; newspapers charge them a specially reduced rate for advertising; European and American girls flock to them as willing volunteers. Although they often present their shows in prestigious concert halls their productions are dismal affairs. The lighting is primitive, the microphone levels are badly set, the stage is seldom used in an imaginative way, the introductions to the various items are either incorrect or incoherent. The Western press and public have a rather superior and patronising attitude towards such amateurishness — "Well, one expects this sort of thing at Indian shows" is a representative remark.

These cultural organizers are doing a disservice to India and yet they enjoy official support. Even well known musicians and dancers, in their keenness to appear abroad, are continually falling into the clutches of these propagators of Indian culture. The artists are paid almost nothing when on tour and their living conditions are often subhuman. Sometimes they are not even fed enough. In one particular instance an established artist refused to go on stage one night because he had not been given a meal during that whole day. Needless to say, the artists themselves are largely to blame for the humiliation meted out to them.

The rush of Indian musicians and dancers to the West in search of success is despicable. One can only hope that, in the course of time, Western audiences will become more discriminating and accept only the best that India has to offer in terms of quality, variety and production. The danger is that before this happens the fashion for things Indian might pass away and then *all* Indian art − good and bad − will be equally ignored. That is why a heavy responsibility rests upon those who set out to interpret India to the West. They must strip away the fashionable and the superficial, the exotic and the pseudo-mystical, and present India in the right perspective, objectively and critically. Only then will there be an abiding appreciation of India's great artistic achievements, and no change in fashions will have any effect upon such an appreciation, for it will have been firmly founded on understanding and truth.

There has been a steady trickle of foreign students going to India in search of musical training. A few of them have made good progress. The Indian government does offer some scholarships to students from abroad but these are, of necessity, limited. There is, however, no reason why the governments of the richer countries should not institute grants and scholarships for this purpose. Europeans and Americans trained by recognized *gurus* in India will be cultural assets to their own countries and will have a favourable influence on their peers at home.

From this let it not be deduced that there are no facilities for learning Indian music in the West. A few universities do offer courses, and some Indian teachers who are resident abroad hold regular classes. It is nevertheless essential for the

There are various types of flute in
India. Here *Vishwanathan*
demonstrates a 'Krishna type' of
flute, or *murli*. The god is reputed to
have been a flute player and is often
depicted with a side-blown instrument.

student to spend time in India if he or she wishes to attain a
reasonable degree of proficiency.

For many years now the East-West musical relationship has
been the object of some careful study. This absorbing subject
was discussed at length in 1964 during an international
conference held at New Delhi. The meeting was sponsored by
the Indian Council for Cultural Relations in association with
the Sangeet Natak Akademi, the Max Müller Bhavan, the
Indian Congress for Cultural Freedom and the Delhi Music
Society. The foreign delegates included the Earl of Harewood,
Yehudi Menuhin, Nicholas Nabokov, Dragotin Cvetko, Alain
Daniélou, Hans Stuckenschmidt, Roger Ashton, Prof. Sychra,
Peter Crossley-Holland, Janos Karpati, Prof. Hacobian, Dr.

Mantle Hood, Prof. Koelreutter, A.E. Spadvekia, Ernest
Meyer, Tran Van Khê, and Dr. Rosette Renshaw. Among the
Indian delegates were Ravi Shankar, Prof. P. Sambamoorthy,
Geeta Mayor, Ali Akbar Khan, Prof. Pant, Prof. Deodhar,
Vilayat Khan, Thakur Jaidev Singh, Amir Khan, Palghat
Mani Iyer, Dr. Kapila Vatsyayan, Bismillah Khan, Dr. R.L.
Roy, Inam Rahman, Heimo Rau, Amarjit Singh, Dr.
Narayana Menon, N.N. Shukla, N.S. Ramachandran,
Charles Fabri and Humayun Kabir.

Many interesting papers were read at this conference but a
speech made by Humayun Kabir upset a number of people in
India. The cause of the furore were the following sentences: "I
do not think that in any realm of human life we can have
closed systems. The fiction of a purely indigenous culture has
been destroyed more effectively today than at any time in the
past. As a student of history, I have never come across any
culture that was pure at any time in the world. In our Indian
languages we have a term called *kitchree*. This means a
medley. Culture must be *kitchree*. In fact it has always been
kitchree, but then the purists came along and worked on it to
try and discover elements of purity which do not exist. Today
that communing is bound to increase. In music as in other
fields where conceptual rigidity is comparatively absent and
where the framework is more fluid and flexible, influences
from other cultures interpenetrate more easily".

The purists of Indian culture were up in arms. For them the
culture of India was a sacred thing, a mystical concept. It had
survived through thousands of years of foreign attack and now,
with political independence, was resplendent in all its pristine
purity. Indeed "pristine purity" is a term greatly loved and often
used by Indian purists. Politically, they are to the extreme
right and their aspirations find expression in organizations of
the most fascist type. They set great store by India's Aryan
past, think highly of Hitler's theories on racial and cultural
purity, and are proud that *swastika* is a pure Sanskrit word. A
particular group of these purists was responsible for the
assassination of Gandhi the man who, above all, brought
about independence in the first place.

Even a cursory study of Indian history makes it abundantly
clear that India has been open to influences from many

quarters and has been conspicuously successful in accommodating and even assimilating them. Indian culture has undergone changes in the process and these, on the whole, have been beneficial. In the area of music, for example, the Islamic impact has been important and about it Bhatkhande wrote, "I am of the opinion that our music gained considerably from the foreign (Muslim) influence".

Kabir, however, had used the word *kitchree*, an unhappy choice for a poet. It means medley only by extension; it is actually a common dish of boiled rice and split pulse. This Hindi word has come into the English language as *kedgeree*. *Kitchree* also means a hodge-podge, a barbarous mixture of two languages, and the earnest money given to a dancing girl. All these are unpleasant connotations, especially when applied to a great culture. What Kabir meant of course was that India's was a *composite* culture and he would have been well advised to have said so.

Zakir Hussein, who has a following in both East and West, has inherited his *tabla* wizardry from his father *Alla Rakha*.

10 *Ragas*

Indian musicologists have written about two kinds of sound, one inaudible to the human ear and one audible, and each was further subdivided. The inaudible sound, *anahata nada*, is described in the *Sangeet-makaranda* as "sound produced from the ether...." "In this unstruck sound the Gods delight. The Yogis, the Great Spirits, projecting their minds by an effort of the mind into this unstruck sound, depart, attaining Liberation". Its function is to liberate and so great is the diligence and devotion it demands in order to be perceived, that most men are neither interested nor delighted by it. The audible sound, *ahata nada*, is "struck" and is said to give pleasure. It is, therefore, that which interests humans.

The word *nada* means sound and derives from *na*, breath, and *da* meaning fire. *Madhura nada* consists of those sounds which are pleasing to the ear; that is, musical sounds or those which have regular vibrations.

Musical sounds are characterized by four main features; namely, pitch, timbre, intensity and duration. Pitch is that property of sound which, depending on the number of vibrations, makes it seem high or low. The timbre is the quality of the sound, and this depends on how it is produced — on the type of instrument or voice. The intensity of the sound is simply its volume. The duration of a sound is the length of time it is held.

In defining the various technical terms used in Indian music the most difficult one to be precise about is the word *sruti* which means "to hear" in Sanskrit. Broadly speaking, the Indian octave, or rather the *saptak* which consists of seven notes instead of the eight of the octave, is divided into 22 intervals. Theoretically, of course, it can be divided into many more and there are musicians in India who insist on 49 intervals, and some even on 66. However, 22 *srutis* are now generally agreed. Although all the intervals are in use, they are not sung or played as a scale, for as such they are purely academic. It can be said that a *sruti*, microtone, does not really have an independent existence and that, while it does have certain characteristics, these are revealed best when the *sruti* is heard within the context of a melodic form.

Alain Daniélou states that it is not possible to sing the scale of 22 *srutis* accurately and undoubtedly the operative word here is "accurately", for there is nothing like absolute agreement on the exact value of each interval. Add to this the

A large trumpet from Himachal Pradesh in north India. Trumpets and horns usually announce village fairs and religious festivals.

fact that each *gharana* has its own peculiarities and it follows that what might be considered accurate by one will be considered quite wrong by another.

An interesting light is thrown on this question by a passage in *Umrao Jan Ada*, a realistic novel by Mirza Ruswa, set during the middle of the last century. The story concerns Umrao Jan, kidnapped as a child and then brought up to be a high class courtesan in Lucknow. These ladies were as skilled in the arts of music, dance and poetry as they were in the manners and customs of the aristocracy. Their training was meticulous and very carefully watched. Umrao Jan goes to visit an older girl who also belongs to the same establishment and whose particular talent is singing. Umrao Jan asks her friend to demonstrate the musical scale. The older girl obliges but Umrao Jan says she didn't hear all the *srutis*. The girl then repeats the performance asking Umrao Jan to count them carefully. The significant point is that she sang only the names of the seven pure, *suddha*, notes, that is, SA, RE, GA, MA, PA, DHA, and NI. Quite obviously Umrao Jan expected to hear the *srutis* as well.

That the training of the girls was carefully watched is borne out by the fact that at one stage the music teacher was sacked for allowing a girl to sing an inappropriate *sruti* in a *raga*.

The 13th century musicologist Sarangadeva had named the 22 *srutis*. Their distribution over the seven notes of the *Sadja-grama*, the parent scale now in use in a modified form, was given in Chapter Four where Sarangadeva's work was discussed.

Bhatkhande realized that for practical purposes Indian music now increasingly relied on the twelve semitones of the Western octave, although there were minor variations from time to time. He therefore worked out a relationship between the semitones and the *srutis*. Since Bhatkhande, further research has considerably clarified this relationship as the following chart on p.95 shows. A *sruti*, therefore, is the smallest division of the *saptak* which is perceptible to the trained and sensitive human ear. Not everyone can hear the *srutis* and one of the disturbing results of the noise that surrounds us today is the reduction in the number of those — even in India — who can hear the *srutis*. During the course of

Western Notes	C	C# or D♭	D	D# or E♭	E	F	F#	G	G# or A♭	A	A# or B♭	B
Indian Notes (*swaras*)	SA	RE♭	RE	GA♭	GA	MA	MA#	PA	DHA♭	DHA	NI♭	NI
Indian Micro-tones (*srutis*)	1	2 3 4	5 6	7	8 9	10	11 12 13	14	15 16 17	18 19	20	21 22
Names of Micro-tones		(1) Tivra (2) Kumadvati (3) Manda (4) Chandovati	(5) Dayavati (6) Ranjini (7) Raktika		(8) Rudri (9) Krodhi		(10) Vajrika (11) Prasarini (12) Priti (13) Marjani		(14) Kshiti (15) Rakta (16) Sandipini (17) Alapini	(18) Madanti (19) Rohini (20) Ramya		(21) Ugra (22) Kshobini

a conversation with us some time ago Ali Akbar Khan expressed grave concern about this matter for, in effect, it endangers the whole future of Indian music. These microtones do not, of course, occur every time Indian music is performed. They are created during rare moments of inspiration when a *gamak*, grace note, richly embellishes a melodic structure. It is while experiencing such a moment that an Indian audience sighs with profound pleasure.

Balachander, the celebrated *veena* player, concentrating on the slow, introductory section of a *raga*. *Balachander* died a few years ago when he was at the height of his powers.

We have already discussed *swaras*, that is those notes which have been sounded long enough to produce expression. In other words, a *swara* is not a soulless or meaningless pitch of sound. It must possess "the capacity to convey an expression to the mind of the hearer". It is, therefore, a pleasing, a musical sound. Of the seven *suddha swaras* two, SA and PA, are *shanta*; they are "at peace" and have no half notes. SA and PA are also known as *acal swaras*, immovable notes, which is a misleading term. RE, GA, DHA, and NI have *komals*, flats, and MA has a *tivra*, sharp. That makes a total of twelve: seven *suddha swaras*, four *komal swaras* and one *tivra swara*. This series of twelve makes up the full scale. Indian musicians often apply the term *vikrit*, altered or modified, to the four *komals* and the one *tivra*.

Kalinath, in his commentary on the *Sangeet-ratnakara*, says that the seven *suddha* notes correspond with the seven basic elements of the body. They have also been called the seven limbs of the modal scale — "The note SA (the tonic) is said to be the soul, RE is called the head, GA the arms, MA the chest, PA the throat, DHA the hips, and NI the feet". Some Sanskrit authorities also assigned to the seven *swaras* colours in the following manner: SA — black, RE — tawny, GA — golden, MA — white, PA — yellow, DHA — purple, and NI — green. They further associated them with castes, connecting SA, MA, and PA with Brahmins, RE and DHA with Kshatriyas, GA and NI with Vaishyas and the *vikrit swaras* with the Shudras.

In the Indian system the tonic, SA, is not fixed at a particular point and may be set in accordance with the convenience of the performer, whether singer or instrumentalist. However, once that is decided upon all the other notes are set in relation to the chosen SA. A movable SA is, of course, impossible when instruments with the tempered or fixed scale are used, and this is the chief objection to the harmonium. This is also a reason, though not the only one, why accurate transcribing in staff notation is impossible and so when staff notation is employed it has more or less become the convention to set SA at middle C. It should at all times be remembered, nevertheless, that this is only a convention.

The question of musical notation has for long been a matter of controversy in India. Some were always against notation on the grounds that it would destroy the intimate teacher-pupil relationship. Others felt that Indian music was too fluid an art form for any system of notation to be either effective or useful. D.N. Tagore invented a type of notation which was later revised by his brother J.N. Tagore. The Tagore system was quite popular until Bhatkhande worked out a simple method that is widely used today. Recently, however, Nikhil Ghosh has devised a new notation which scripts Indian music accurately and fairly easily. The Ghosh system deserves greater acceptance; certainly among Hindustani musicians.

The well known Pakistani vocalists *Salamat Ali Khan* (left) and his elder brother, the late *Nazakat Ali Khan*.

Given below are some well known *ragas*. The notations only provide the ascending and descending note patterns with, for convenience, the Western C representing the Indian SA:

Bahar

Bhairav

Bhairavi

Sindhi Bhairavi

Bhimpalashri

Darbari Kannada

Darbari

Desh

Hamsadvani

Jaijaivanti

Khamaj

Megh Malhar

Pilu

Shyam Kalyani

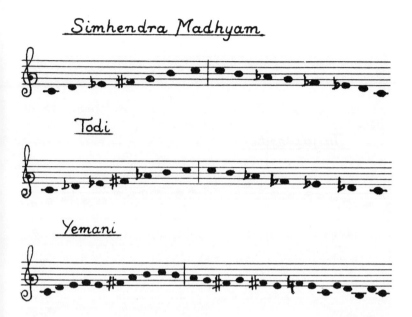

In Indian music there are generally three registers called *sthans*. The *mandra* is the low register corresponding to the bass; the *madhya* is the middle register; and the *tar* corresponds to the treble. A very low register, *ati-mandra*, is sometimes used by instrumentalists and on rare occasions one hears a very high or *ati-tar* register.

The *ragas* are derived from basic parent scales. In south India these are known as *melakartas*. There are seventy-two *melakartas* and all the south Indian *ragas* correspond to their parent scales in their ascending, *aroha*, and descending, *avroha*, note structure. This is a more comprehensive system than that which exists in north India where there are ten parent groups known as *thaats*.

Nowadays a few musicians from north India, such as Ravi Shankar, prefer to use the *melakarta* classification. Others have modified the ten *thaat* system to suit their requirements. Most, however, still use the ten *thaats* first propounded by Bhatkhande. The great musicologist was aware of the fact that a thirty-two *thaat* grouping would be more precise. Nevertheless, having introduced the ten *thaats*, he was reluctant to rush in with yet another innovation. In 1971, N.A. Jairazbhoy provided a scientific basis for a thirty-two *thaat* system while, at the same time, proving the inadequacies of the present ten *thaats*. Jairazbhoy has made a powerful plea but it is too early to assess the reactions of practising musicians in India.

In the meantime, Bhatkhande's ten accepted *thaats* are as follows:

NAME OF THAAT	NOTES						
1 Bilaval	SA	RE	GA	MA	PA	DHA	NI
2 Kalyan	SA	RE	GA	MA#	PA	DHA	NI
3 Khamaj	SA	RE	GA	MA	PA	DHA	NI♭
4 Bhairav	SA	RE♭	GA	MA	PA	DHA♭	NI
5 Purvi	SA	RE♭	GA	MA#	PA	DHA♭	NI
6 Marva	SA	RE♭	GA	MA#	PA	DHA	NI
7 Kafi	SA	RE	GA♭	MA	PA	DHA	NI♭
8 Asavari	SA	RE	GA♭	MA	PA	DHA♭	NI♭
9 Bhairavi	SA	RE♭	GA♭	MA	PA	DHA♭	NI♭
10 Todi	SA	RE♭	GA♭	MA#	PA	DHA♭	NI

Bhatkhande named these *thaats* after well known *ragas* only to facilitate recognition. Under *Bilaval thaat*, for instance, there is *Raga Bilaval* and a number of other *ragas* of the same type. So also with the other *thaats*.

As can be seen, a *thaat* is simply a particular grouping of seven *swaras* in their order of succession and does not have *swara varna*, that is, ascending or descending runs of notes. Also, it never incorporates the *suddha* and *vikrit* of the same note. It has no colour of its own but is merely a base from which *ragas* of a particular colour and character are derived. The *thaat* itself is related to the *murchana*, or mode, used in ancient times before the *raga* had evolved.

An Indian ensemble at London's Queen Elizabeth Hall. In the middle sits the *jaltarang* player

Whereas a *thaat* is a combination of notes without any particular appeal, a *raga* must be aesthetically pleasing. The word comes from the Sanskrit *ranj*, to colour with emotion. A *raga*, therefore, must "dye the mind in colour". It must have a distinct character, a sentiment.

Ragas belong to three classes or *jatis* according to the number of notes used in ascent and descent. *Sampūrna* means "complete" and a *raga* so called uses all the seven notes of the scale in ascent and descent. *Bilaval* and *Kafi* are examples of *sampūrna ragas*. *Ragas* which use six notes are known as *sādava* and examples of these are *Puriya* and *Gurjari Todi*. The five note *ragas* such as *Bhupali* and *Malkauns* are *odava*. In addition to these three main types, *ragas* may be of mixed class where the number of notes in ascent and descent are different. *Asavari*, for example, is an *odava-sampūrna raga* as it has five notes in the ascent (*aroha*) and seven in the descent (*avroha*). However, a *raga* may not have more than seven or less than five notes. There are exceptions to this rule which do not really matter.

Every *raga* has a note known as the *vadi*. This is dwelt on and accentuated constantly throughout the exposition and is used to begin and end all variations. Since it is the one note most often played in a *raga* it is also the note which gives a *raga* its main expression. In variations it is eagerly desired and awaited in order that tension may be resolved. It was originally called the *amsa*, keynote.

The function of the subdominant note, *samvadi*, is to reinforce the *vadi*. It is always a fourth or a fifth from the *vadi*. The other notes of a *raga* are called *anuvadi*.

Notes which are contrary to the mood or character of a *raga* and which would destroy its overall effect are known as *vivadi*, or dissonant, and are to be avoided. However, masters of their art do, on occasion, briefly refer to a note which is *vivadi* in order to create a special effect without interfering with the main mood of the *raga*.

Another important feature of a *raga* is its *pakad* which means "that whereby one can lay hold". In other words, it is a catch phrase by which a *raga* can immediately be identified. However, a clear picture of a *raga* only emerges when there is an elaboration of a number of patterns. This is called *vistar*.

Earlier we referred to the *aroha* and *avroha*; the ascending and descending motions of a *raga*. Sometimes the same phrase occurs repeatedly and this theme fixing section is known as *sthayi*. When these three features are "mixed" they are collectively termed *sanchari*. Since a *raga* is essentially a melody archetype all notes are sung or played in succession and there is no harmony. Therefore, *sanchari* does not imply more than one note at a time.

Ali Akbar Khan, the great *sarod* player.

Indeed, the movement from one note to another is what distinguishes Indian music from Western music. In Indian music the transition is always affected by a delicate hint, a nuance. Plentiful use is made of *gamaks*, grace notes. Somnatha gave fifty examples of *gamaks* in his *Ragavibodha*, (1609). He wrote, "... a melody devoid of embellishments is like a moonless night, a river without water, a creeper without flowers or a woman without a garment".

A *raga* is given body, spread out, and beautified by numerous ornaments, *alamkaras*, and other devices, the best known of which are the *taans*. The *jabra taan* creates a trembling, throaty effect; the *kut taan* uses notes in a fast zig-zag manner; the *choot taan* has upward and downward movements at great speed; the *gamak taan* uses each note twice in virtuoso displays of technique. There is also a vast variety of embellishments such as *meends*, slides, *andolitas*, swings, *kampitas*, shakes, and *mirhs*, slurs.

A *raga* expresses a sentiment. Since the notes themselves are considered to have their own evocative power, the mood of the *raga* is the result of the choice of notes comprising the scale. This prevailing mood is made possible and sustained by the fact that Indian music, like Scottish and Irish music is modal and not harmonic. It exists by the relation of the notes to each other and especially to the tonic and dominant which must, like the drone of the bagpipes, be ever-present in the background or, failing this, sounded frequently. During a performance it is this mood, colour or passion which the musician tries to evoke and explore, and according to ancient theory his task is made easier if the performance takes place at the time and in the *ambiance* proper to the *raga*. If, for example, a *raga* which embodies the atmosphere of spring is played in springtime, it will be more effective than if it is played in winter. The right atmosphere responds to the *raga* as it were, just as the sympathetic strings of a *sitar* vibrate to and enrich the melody being played on the main strings. This is why particular times and seasons are deemed suitable for particular *ragas*.

The time theory is an honoured one in all Indian classical music. There are *ragas* appropriate to the early morning, the late morning, the noon and afternoon, the evening, the early night, the deep night, and the late night. Then there are seasonal *ragas* as, for example, *Vasanta* for the spring and *Miyañ-ki-Malhar* for the rainy season.

In general, the time of a *raga's* performance is determined by the position of its *vadi*. If the *vadi* is in the *purvanga* (lower tetrachord) then it would be suitable for the hours between midday and midnight; if the dominant note lies in the *uttranga* (upper tetrachord) it would be suitable for the hours between midnight and midday. Midday and midnight *ragas* usually have GA♭ (E♭) and NI♭ (B♭); and the *ragas* before twilight must have SA (C), MA (F), and PA (G).

Nikhil Ghosh writes, "Just as the rising sun, whose light emerges from darkness, has an effect different from that of the setting sun, where darkness follows light, so also RE *komal* (D♭) emerging from SA (C), has an effect different from RE *komal* going back to SA. At dawn there is a very gradual diffusion of light from darkness; similarly, at dusk, of darkness from light. It is at these hours that *komal swaras* are appropriate". Indeed, these *ragas* of the sunrise and the sunset belong to the special *sandhiprakash*, twilight, group.

Let us now endeavour to describe what happens during a recital of Indian music.

Tabla virtuoso *Alla Rakha.*

To Occidentals used to the rich textures of harmony, lack of it or virtual lack of it, combined with an inescapable drone, must seem intolerably tedious. The seeming lack of variety will disappear only if the listener learns to look for what is there rather than search in vain for something that simply does not exist.

What, then, is the special quality of Indian music?

The Indian musician-composer, for that is what every Indian musician really is, seeks unity and eschews diversity, which may be distracting. His aim is to reveal the purity of each note and to bring out the full flavour of the *bhava*, mood, or *rasa*, emotional state, he is trying to create. To this end he does not consciously use harmony. For him, two or more notes played together serve only to obscure the purity of each single note; instead he plays *gamaks*, grace notes, which are very close to the main note on either side. He never plays a bare, unadorned note but embellishes it with a slide in either direction. This is contrary to Western practice where portamento is avoided — curiously enough for the same reason, that is, purity.

In Indian music there is always a constant drone in the background. This serves as a continual point of reference and as a guide, and is regarded as absolutely indispensable.

Indian music does not so much describe a mood — as does European music — as create it, explore it, and try to plumb its depths. Where Western music starts at a particular point and then progresses from it, Indian music revolves round it, probing it and examining it from every possible angle. There is no question of progressing away from it.

In a full rendering of a *raga* the most important part is the *alap*, the beginning, when the mood of the *raga* is established in a slow, meditative and rhythm-free exposition, known as the *vistar*, where each note is given full significance. In the *jorh* and *jhala* an element of rhythm is brought in, but still without the percussion instrument. The *raga* is now developed further and explored in complex variations. The percussion instrument, usually the *tabla* or *pakhavaj* in north India and the *mridangam* in south India, joins the main instrument for the last section of the performance. Here rhythm is all important, and both percussionist and soloist improvise,

Ravi Shankar

sometimes echoing each other, sometimes going into individual variations of rhythmic counterpoint, and at other times playing in unison. This last part, the *gath*, may begin in a slow tempo, *vilambit*, and then increase to a medium, *madhya*, and finally to a fast tempo, *drut*. The virtuosity of the musicians is fully displayed here, and the increasing complexity and speed of the variations generate tremendous excitement.

11 *Talas*

Just as the *ragas* organize melody so *talas* organize rhythm. Indian music has highly developed and sophisticated rhythmic structures and these are manifest in *talas*, time measures. The word *tala* seems to have at least two sources. It is said to derive from *tali*, clap, since the measures have to be clapped out by hand. The other source, more elevated, concerns the god Shiva and his consort Parvati. Shiva's dance was *tandav*, masculine, and Parvati's was *lasya*, feminine. The *ta* from *tandav* and the *la* from *lasya* make up *tala*.

In theory there are hundreds of *talas* ranging from 3 to 108 beats, but percussionists today use about thirty to forty types. *Talas* have certain distinctive features, and we shall consider each feature separately.

The *matras* are the beats which make up a *tala*. For example, *teental*, also called *tritala*, has 16 *matras*; *jhumra* has 14 *matras*, and *dadra* only 6. The question now arises: What is the time value of a *matra*? This, of course, depends upon the speed of play, the tempo. However, the Indian sages of the past argued that as the "natural tempo" of a healthy man was the rate of his pulse beat, therefore, the duration of the ideal *matra* must also be of the same time value. Since the pulse beats 70 to 80 times a minute we can assume that the ideal *matra* has a duration of between 6/7 of a second and 3/4 of a second. This length of time is known as the *anudrut*.

Half a *matra* is a *truti*, a quarter of a *matra* a *kalā*, and one-eighth of a *matra* is equal to four *nimesas*. Divisions of less than one-eighth of a *matra* are, however, hardly ever played. Apart from this, the *matra's* duration can also be divided up into three parts, five parts, seven parts, and so on.

The time value of two *matras* is called a *drut*, of four a *laghu*, of eight a *guru*, of twelve a *pluta* and of sixteen a *kakapada*.

Laya is the term for tempo. There are seven recognized tempi: *ati-vilambit*, very slow; *vilambit*, slow; *madhya vilambit*, medium slow; *madhya*, medium; *madhya drut*, medium fast; *drut*, fast; and *ati-drut*, very fast. The "natural tempo" of 70 to 80 *matras* a minute is regarded as *vilambit laya*; twice this speed is *madhya laya*; and four times the speed of *vilambit laya* is known as *drut laya*. The other four tempi are relative to these.

Angas or *vibhags* are the limbs or parts into which a *tala* is usually divided. They are, in effect, bars. *Teental*, for instance, has 16 *matras* divided into four *angas*, each with four *matras*.

The most unfamiliar aspect of *tala* to the Western ear is that the cycle ends not, as might be expected, on the last beat of the measure but on the first beat of the next cycle. This first is the most important beat of the *tala* and is known as the *sum*. It bears the heaviest stress and around it the whole rhythm cycle revolves. It serves as a signpost both of the beginning and of the end. All variations end on the *sum* and performers often indicate it by nodding to each other when they arrive on it, thus signifying satisfaction and appreciation. The *sum* is a point of culmination which completes a rhythmic structure.

The other important beats are called *talis* and are shown by claps, while the ordinary accented beats are counted with the fingers of the right hand on to the palm of the left. The *khalis* ("empties") are the unstressed beats and are indicated by a short sideways wave of the right hand, palm upwards. The *khalis* serve a vital purpose in that they are points of contrast and, at the same time, help to place the *sum* and the *talis*.

Indian musicians use a time honoured system of mnemonics consisting of a large number of recited syllables. Every percussionist must master these *boles* and their variations. Celebrated artists like Palghat Mani Iyer, the *mridangam* player, and Alla Rakha, the *tabla* player, have invented their own variations at different tempi. Most percussionists also convey mood and feeling through their playing of different *talas. Dhamar*, for example, can produce a vigorous feeling while *dadra* evokes a romantic mood.

Here are a few *talas*. A cross marks the *sum*, and a zero shows the *khali*.

TEENTAL or TRITALA

TALIS (important beats)	**✝** 1				2				0				3			
MATRAS (beats)	1	2	3	4	5	6	7	8	9	10	11	12	13	14	15	16
BOLES (recited syllables)	dha	dhin	dhin	dha	dha	dhin	dhin	dha	dha	thin	thin	tha	tha	dhin	dhin	dha
ANGAS (bars)	I				II				III				IV			

Teental, it will be seen, has 16 *matras*, divided 4-4-4-4. There are three stresses: on *matra* 1 (the *sum*), 5, and 13. *Matra* 9 is the *khali*.

Teental has been popular for two centuries and over the years many fixed compositions in this *tala* have been established.

JHUMRA

TALIS (important beats)	**✝** 1			2				0			3			
MATRAS (beats)	1	2	3	4	5	6	7	8	9	10	11	12	13	14
BOLES (recited syllables)	dhin	dha	tere-kete	dhin	dhin	dhage	tere-kete	thin	tha	tere-kete	dhin	dhin	dhage	tere-kete
ANGAS (bars)	I			II				III			IV			

Jhumra is often used for *Khayals*.

DHAMAR

TALIS (important beats)	**+** 1			0		2		0			3		0	
MATRAS (beats)	1	2	3	4	5	6	7	8	9	10	11	12	13	14
BOLES (recited syllables)	ka	dhi	ta	dhi	ta	dha	rest for one matra	ghe	ti	ta	ti	ta	ta	rest for one matra
ANGAS (bars)	I			II		III		IV			V		VI	

Dhamar presents an interesting case. Firstly, there is a difference of opinion regarding the divisions. Above we have 3-2-2-3-2-2. Some percussionists divide it 5-5-4 and others 5-2-3-4. *Talas* quite often have different *matra* groupings, *angas*, depending upon particular *gharana* conventions. Secondly, it has two rest *matras*; so that although there are 14 *matras* the number of *boles* is 12.

In some *talas* there could be a half rest *matra* with the remaining half indicated by a short *bole*.

Dhamar tala is used for *Dhamar* songs which tell of the god Krishna during the spring festival of Holi.

Rupak is a popular *tala* and one of the most controversial. In the notation overleaf, the *khali* occupies the usual position of the *sum*. According to some musicians the *khali* is so unstressed that it serves the purpose of the *sum*: a contradiction in terms since, by definition, the *sum* bears the heaviest accent. However, we must accept the view of practising musicians and reject the diametrically opposite theory of at least two musicologists that *rupak* has no *khali* at all. (For diagrams of *Rupak* and *Dadra*, see overleaf).

Dadra is named after the *Dadra* song types for which this time measure is normally employed.

The basic percussion phrases which identify *talas* are called *thekas*, and variations of *thekas* are known as *parans*. These variations are usually developed when a percussionist gives a

RUPAK

TALIS (important beats)	0			1		2	
MATRAS (beats)	1	2	3	4	5	6	7
BOLES (recited syllables)	thin	thin	na	dhi	na	dhi	na
ANGAS (bars)	I			II		III	

DADRA

TALIS (important beats)	**+** 1			0		
MATRAS (beats)	1	2	3	4	5	6
BOLES (recited syllables)	dha	dhin	na	dha	thin	na
ANGAS (bars)	I			II		

solo performance. South Indian drummers, however, have their *tala vadya kacheris*, ensembles for percussion instruments. During such performances a variety of drums are used in a series of solos and exciting competitive drumming, with — at the end — a marvellous torrent of rhythm by all the drummers playing in unison. Under Ravi Shankar's inspiration north India has taken up this idea and now Hindustani and Karnatic percussionists often perform together. The language of rhythm overcomes the limitations of the spoken tongue.

12 Music and the Allied Arts

Bharata, the father of Indian aesthetics, saw all artistic forms as expressions of the same creative urge. They were all, therefore, connected. Music, however, has a special position in the hierarchy of art since sound was a vital factor in the very creation of the Universe. In the beginning was the Word. When one considers the famous figure of Shiva as Nataraj, the creator, the preserver, the destroyer, and the Lord of the Dance, one sees how well the ancient Hindus understood the primacy of sound. In his right hand the god holds the *damru*, small drum, the symbol of creation.

The idea of creation by means of sound has its roots in the belief that there are two kinds of sound. The struck, *ahata*, is audible to us but the unstruck, *anahata*, is unaudible. Only those few humans who have attained the highest levels of consciousness can hear unstruck sound which gives them complete liberation from this world and makes them one with the cosmos. In the same way, with the Pythagorean theory, the music of the spheres could not normally be heard by humans. Whereas the sound we hear dies away, the other "forms permanent numerical patterns which lie at the very root of the world's existence". It is "the principle of all manifestation and the basis of all substance".

Shiva first played the *damru* and then — to the beats of the drum — he performed his dance of creation. Thus, from the very beginning, an intimate relationship was formed between the arts of music and dance.

Technically, it is the *talas* which bind the dancer to the musician. *Nritta*, pure dance, would be impossible without rhythm. there are moments in a *Bharata Natyam* performance when the *nattuvanar,* dance teacher, recites certain syllables in particular rhythmic patterns. These are purely dance syllables and have no meaning, and are known as *sollukuttus.* The *nattuvanar* beats out the rhythm of the syllables on his small brass cymbals and the dancer duplicates them with the bells on her ankles.

A brilliant succession of dance units is known as a *tirmana.* These *tirmanas* are danced to complex patterns known as *jatis.* There are five types of *jatis,* based on 3, 4, 5, 7 and 9 beats. *Tisra jati* is the first type and has the syllables ta-ki-ta. The second type, the *chaturasra,* of four beats is ta-ka-dhi-mi. The third, *khanda jati,* has five beats which are ta-ka ta-ki-ta. The seven beats of the *misra jati* are ta-ka-dhi-mi ta-ki-ta. The fifth type which has nine beats, ta-ka-dhi-mi ta-ka ta-ki-ta, is the *sankirna jati.*

The syllables of a *jati* are vocal representations of the sounds which the dancer has to produce from her ankle bells by striking the stage with her feet. She can do this by bringing her foot down flat or striking only with the heel or toe.

Jatis played on the drums are called *chollus.*

The expressionistic portions of *Bharata Natyam* consist of *shabdams,* danced songs, or *padams,* danced love lyrics. It was originally intended that the dancer herself should sing when performing a *padam,* but not all dancers do this today, although some may occasionally join in with the musician or even take over the singing. Most of the love lyrics are in Tamil, Telugu or Sanskrit and they have all developed into poems of seven lines from short Sanskrit verses called *slokas.*

The *Kathak* dance style of north India has a highly developed and complex technique of footwork. The skill of the dancer and percussionist is judged by the accuracy with which, after complicated variations, they arrive simultaneously at the *sum.* A variation is usually spread over several bars and the excitement reaches a climax with the first beat of the next cycle. The dancer and musician memorize the *boles,* rhythmic syllables, with the help of a system of clapping. However, the dance *boles* and the *tabla boles* are different. An example of the first set of *boles* in *teental* is given on the next page.

These are the sixteen *boles* of the *tabla* which correspond to

TALIS (important beats)	**+** 1	2	0	3
TABLA BOLES	dha dhin dhin dha 1▪ 2 3 4	dha dhin dhin dha 5 6 7 8	dha thin thin tha 9 10 11 12	tha dhin dhin dha 13 14 15 16
DANCE BOLES	**+** tha a thei ee ‿ ‿ 1 2	thé ee tha th ‿ ‿ 3 4	aa a thé ee ‿ ‿ 5 6	thé ee tha th ‿ ‿ 7 8

the eight *boles* of the dance. The diagram makes it clear that, for every two *tabla* beats there is just one dance beat. In both cases three beats are important. For the *tabla boles* these are the first (marked +) which is the *sum*, the fifth, and the thirteenth. The corresponding stressed dance beats are, the first, again the *sum*, the third, and the seventh. The ninth *tabla* beat, which in the case of the dance is the fifth beat, is the *khali* or empty (marked 0).

Nritya, the expression of sentiment and mood in dance, is also an important aspect of *Kathak*. It is usual for *nritya* items to be named after the styles of singing in which the words are rendered; so that there are *Dhrupads, Keertans, Dadras* and *Ghazals*. When performing any of these the dancer is normally expected to do the singing as well. Another type of *nritya* in this dance is the manner in which a *Thumri* may be rendered. Here the interpretation of the poem is of prime importance and the accompanying *bhava* (delineation of emotions and feelings) is so delicate that footwork would be a distracting element. It is, therefore, excluded. The dancer sits with a shawl draped over the legs and feet. The *bhava* is rendered mainly by the face, the eyes in particular. The hands and body play a secondary rôle. The performer repeatedly sings a line of the poem, interpreting it differently each time with corresponding changes in *bhava* and so exploits every shade of meaning. The greater the performer the more variations he presents. Maharaj Binda Din, a famous dancer of the last century who was at the court of Nawab Wajid Ali Shah of Lucknow, is said to have interpreted a single line from a poem about the god Krishna from dusk to dawn without ever duplicating a variation or a nuance. A rendering in this manner is known as *Thumri Andaaz.*

In recent years one of the finest artists of *Thumri Andaaz* was the late Shambu Maharaj, a nephew of Maharaj Binda Din. He had a wide repertoire and one of his favourite *Thumris* was "Bata do guniyaṅ, kaun galiṅ gayo Shyam?" which means "Do tell me, dear friend, which way has Shyam gone?"

"Galiṅ" means "lane", and "Shyam" is another epithet of Krishna as the Dark One.

Shambu Maharaj sang this line several times, underlining a particular word or syllable in each rendering. His face and eyes displayed the *bhavas*, and *hastas*, hand gestures, assisted in their expression. The acting brought to life metaphors, images, similes and metaphysical conceits which were not explicit in the poem. For example, he showed Radha applying *surma* or kohl to the lower eyelid as an eye-liner. The movement of her finger was the lane and the black *surma* symbolic of Krishna the Dark One. In another sense this could mean "Shyam has entered my soul as the *surma* enters my eye".

The line was repeated. Radha was preparing to meet Krishna; she combed her hair and as the dark tresses were loosened she associated them with the Dark One. As she plaited her hair the plait itself became suggestive of the lane.

With the next repetition Radha was seen applying *sindhoor*, a red powder, in the parting of her hair and Krishna was represented as entering her heart as the *sindhoor* entered the parting.

In yet another instance she was searching for Krishna and the dark clouds gathering overhead, heavy with monsoon passion, filled her with desire for her dark lover.

Varying the image again, Radha opened a phial of *attar*. She dabbed some on the back of her hand and inhaled the perfume. Just as the sweet scent gratified her senses, so Krishna entered and uplifted her soul.

His renderings showed that Shambu Maharaj had the sensibility of a poet and it was this which enabled him to interpret and express the sentiments implicit in the poem. He extended the significance of each one by adding to it from his own creative imagination.

Like the Indian musician who has to be an impromptu composer as well, a performer of *Thumri Andaaz* too must be an inspired poet of gestures that suggest and explore different levels of meaning.

Several *Thumris* danced today are the compositions of Maharaj Binda Din who was a devotee of Krishna. Both *Thumris* and *Bhajans* were very often addressed to Krishna in terms of human love. This convention is sometimes followed in *Ghazals* and *Qawwalis* as well and since these are in the Islamic tradition they are addressed to God. The idea is not unique and there are numerous examples of it in Donne and some of his contemporaries. For instance, here is a stanza from Francis Quarles the seventeenth-century English metaphysical poet:

"Why dost thou shade they lovely face? O why
Does that ecclipsing hand, so long, deny
The sunshine of thy soul-enliv'ning eye?"

This might almost be a translation of a *Bhajan* addressed to Krishna by the poetess Mira and exactly the kind of song that made excellent *nritya* material.

We have specifically dealt with *Bharata Natyam* and *Kathak* here: the one from the south, angled and sculptured; the other from the north, fluid and charged with lightning movement. In both cases music and poetry form an integral part of the final artistic product. This, however, is so with every Indian dance style, be it classical or folk.

From Bharata's writing it is quite clear that the drama of his time employed music and dance as a matter of course. Sanskrit drama often took the form of a dance opera and much of the folk drama in India today is of this type. In early Hindu plays music, poetry, dance and costume were equal members of the same body and it is no mere coincidence that Indian films with the widest appeal tend to use that formula. Without being conscious of it the popular movie makers, though not producing "art", have become the heirs of the great Sanskrit dramatists.

Indian temples are literally covered with sculptures and friezes of musicians and dancers. The most celebrated of these is the great temple at Chidambaram which is dedicated to

Shiva Nataraj. Legend has it that the god himself laid the
foundation of the temple, but in fact construction started
around 600 A.D. and over the centuries various dynasties of
kings have made renovations and additions. The gateways or
gopurams of the temple are adorned with bas-reliefs of dancers
and musicians. These constitute, as it were, sermons in stone
for the dance creator and musicologist of today.

Other important examples of this type of art can be seen at
Elura (7th-8th century), Kancipuram (8th century), Aihole
(10th century), Bhuvaneshvara (11th century), Bidar (11th
century), Ujjain (11th century), Raichur (12th century),

Sculptures of musicians and dancers adorn most Indian
temples. This fine example of a female drummer is from
Konarak in Orissa.

Palampet (13th century), Srisailam (13th-14th century), and Puspagiri (14th century).

In the twelfth century came the rise of Vaishnavism, the cult of the god Vishnu especially in his incarnation as Krishna. It spread from the north and had an immediate appeal wherever it went. People turned to it as a more comprehensible expression of their faith and many temples were dedicated to it. Of the Vaishnavite temples those at Belur and Halebid have a special significance for music and dance. They are, of course, decorated with sculptures of Vishnu and the many legends about him, but they also keep alive the name of a very remarkable queen. This royal lady, Queen Santala, is said to have been a famous dancer and musician, and it was in the black marble-pillared halls of these temples that she performed eight hundred years ago. Sculptures depicting her are among the most beautiful there, and have been a constant source of inspiration to succeeding generations of artists.

The religion of the Buddha started as an austere and puritanical way of life. Later, however, the arts were cultivated and evidence of this can be seen in the marvellous cave temples of Ajanta, the earliest of which date from the first century B.C. The classic wall painting of the Great Bodhisattva ("One capable of supreme knowledge or Buddhahood") reveals particularly well the relationship between music, dance and painting. The body rests in the *tribhanga,* a pose much used by dancers, which involves a harmonious curve with three bends in the body. The *mudra,* hand gesture, is clearly taken from the dancer's vocabulary and the whole figure is vibrant with rhythm as if on the point of starting another movement.

There are other murals of musicians, dancing girls and *apsaras,* celestial nymphs. In cave after cave the monk-painters were able to sustain the feel and theme of music and movement. Ajanta is an artistic triumph which has miraculously survived the ravages of time.

Centuries after Ajanta, Indian artists began to produce *raga-ragini* paintings. These works, by painters of the Mughal, Rajput, Deccani, Pahari and other schools, endeavoured to convey the mood of music through the medium of paint. The central figures in these paintings were often Radha and

"Gunakali ragini" (Bundi, c1680) (courtesy of the
Victoria & Albert Museum)

Krishna or a prince and princess. An appropriate poem was usually inscribed on the painting together with the name of the *raga* or *ragini* which was being illustrated. The colours, the symbols, and the images were all subtly used to create the atmosphere of the music.

As an example, let us describe a *Gunakali ragini* painting from the Rajput school.

There is a mood of sensual expectation as the mistress awaits her lover who is late. She holds a cup of *attar* in her left hand and with her right she perfumes the leaves of two potted plants in the courtyard. She is bedecked with ornaments and her skin has a blue colour from the ashes that she has, in the past, applied to her voluptuous body. This she did to make her sorrow evident, and it also signifies separation and despair. The sky is turbulent and reflects her restlessness. But there is hope for we can see two pairs of birds among the flowering trees while a beautiful peacock is in the process of killing a dangerous centipede. There is no doubt that the lover will arrive but we, like the mistress who has pined for months, are just a little uneasy. It is this tantalizing quality of suggestive nuance that never fails to charm and delight.

The *raga-ragini* painters were able, with the help of generally accepted symbolic conventions, to evoke the finest shades of meaning and emotion. They, with the brush, created music just as their musical colleagues painted pictures with sound.

13   Indian Music and the East

The Hindu colonization of south-east Asia has had a lasting effect on the cultures of countries such as Laos, Cambodia, Viet-Nam, Thailand, and Indonesia. The island of Bali, for instance, has preserved its Hindu culture with an enthusiasm that is lacking in many parts of India itself, and in Malaysia the ancient and popular art of shadow puppetry, *Wayang Kulit*, takes all its subject matter from the epics of India. The term "Indo-China" (*Hind-Chine* in Hindi) is an indication of Indian influence in that part of the world. The musical culture of south-east Asia is largely of Hindu origin even though in countries like Viet-Nam the music of China has made a permanent impression.

Indian missionaries carried the Buddha's teachings to every corner of Asia and with them went, quite incidentally, Indian literature, art and music. Buddhism made its greatest impact on China and, later, it spread to Korea and Japan. Buddhist themes and philosophical ideas have, in the past, deeply influenced the painting, sculpture, music and dance of these three countries. It must be said, however, that traditional music is fast dying out in the countries of east Asia. Orchestral music of the Western type has ousted the folk and classical types. Even their traditional instruments have been redesigned to accommodate the Western system of equal temperament, and most musicians now refer to absolute pitch. In China all players of wind instruments have adopted the universal standard pitch, that is, with a tuning note of A. The musicologist Tran Van Khê, in a paper published in the *Unesco Courier* of June 1973, traces the history of this Western musical imperialism and warns of the dangers that lie ahead. Unless a real and conscious effort is made to revive the musical cultures of south-east and east Asia the future seems bleak indeed.

Improvisation, so essential to Indian music, is no longer encouraged or appreciated in China, Korea and south-east Asia. In Japan it has ceased to exist.

India's musical connections with west Asia have been mentioned in a previous chapter. The musical systems of Iran, Arabia, Turkey, Greece, north Africa and the Celtic countries have always been — like Indian music — of a modal, non-harmonic character. Bharata, in fact, refers to Greek and Turkish music.

The *saw-u* of Thailand (courtesy of the Information Service of Thailand)

At this point it would be appropriate to describe the rôle of the earliest emigrants from the Indian subcontinent, namely, the wandering tribes of gipsies. These people have been called *gipsies* in English for no other reason than that when they first appeared in England, in the 16th century, it was believed that they had come from Egypt. *Gipcyan* in those days was the word for Egyptian. They are, however, a race of Hindu origin who speak a corrupted form of Hindi. From India they took with them a love of animals bordering on veneration, an interest in fortune-telling and a passion for music. They have a marvellous facility for adopting the religion, names, and way of life of the country in which they happen to be. They have, also, imparted an Indian sensibility to whatever music they have adapted. When, for example, they entered Spain in the mid-15th century they took the Andalusian *cante hondo* and gave it a peculiar fire and wildness. Later these adaptations, by the gipsies and those who emulated them, came to be called *cante flamenco*. This type of song is reminiscent of Indian singing. Flamenco dance, moreover, clearly exhibits some features of *Kathak*.

The Muslim period of Indian history was, in a curious way, an important time for the export of Indian music. The Muslim princes were related to, or had diplomatic relations with, Muslim rulers in other countries. One of the ways in which they could demonstrate their goodwill was by sending out musicians and dancers to friendly courts, and the area in which such cultural delegations operated was enormous since Islam once held sway from southern France to the islands of Indonesia.

Dilshad Khan and *Parveen Sultana* are widely regarded as the most exciting vocalists of the Hindustani style today.

14   The Instruments

There are four types of instruments, *vadya*, used in Indian music: *Tantu*, stringed; *Susir*, wind; *Avanada*, percussion; and *Ghana*, gongs, bells and cymbals.

TANTU VADYA

Sitar
The *sitar* owes its origin to Amir Khusro who lived in the 13th century. The instrument's name is derived from the Persian *'seh-tar'*, 'three-stringed'. It belongs to the lute family and is made from a seasoned gourd, which acts as a resonating chamber, and teakwood. There are six or seven main strings (four of which are played and two or three used as drone and rhythm strings) and from eleven to nineteen sympathetic strings, the two sets being carried on separate bridges. Twenty frets made of brass and tied to the long hollow neck with string can easily be moved in order to conform to the scale of a particular *raga*. The main strings, which are tuned, are plucked with a *mizrab*, plectrum, worn on the index finger of the right hand. The sympathetic strings are also tuned and usually vibrate to the sound of the main strings. They are, however, plucked on occasion by the little finger of the right hand inserted between the main strings.

Sitars are of varying sizes, the smaller ones often played by women. Some have an extra gourd at the end of the neck.

The most popular stringed instrument among Hindustani musicians, the *sitar*, is also the best known Indian instrument abroad.

Surbahar

The *surbahar* is in effect a bass *sitar* and is played in a similar manner. The resonating chamber again consists of a gourd but in this case the gourd instead of being sliced downwards, as in the *sitar*, is cut across the top so that the back is flat. The neck is wider and longer than that of the *sitar* but its frets are fixed. Thus, because the instrument is larger and has longer strings the sound can be held much longer and this quality is further enhanced by pulling the strings across the frets, at a right angle to the neck and so raising the pitch. In addition to its six metal strings, of which four carry the melody and two the drone, and thirteen sympathetic strings underneath, the *surbahar* has two extra bass strings which give an extra lower octave. Because the *surbahar* produces a deep, dignified sound it lends itself to the *alap, jorh* and *jhala* of a *raga*.

Surbahar means 'melody of Spring' and the instrument was

developed by Sahibdad Khan, the great-grandfather of Vilayat and Imrat Khan.

Sarod
The *sarod* was developed from the *rabab* of Afghanistan. Ustad Allauddin Khan improved the *sarod* and it was his masterly handling of the instrument that led to an increase in

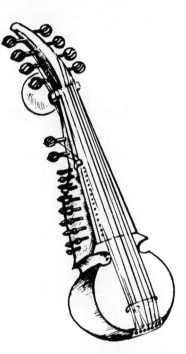

its popularity. Smaller than a *sitar*, it has two resonating chambers. The larger of these is made of teak and covered with goatskin and the smaller at the other end of the unfretted, tapering fingerboard is, like the fingerboard itself, made of metal. Of its twenty-five metal strings, fifteen are sympathetic and lie underneath the ten playing strings. These are plucked with a coconut shell and four of them carry the melody, two or three accentuate the rhythm and the rest are tuned to the dominant note of the chosen *raga*. These side strings also act as the drone.

Sarangi

The *sarangi* is a fretless stringed instrument played with a bow. The whole body — belly and fingerboard — is carved out of a single block of wood and the hollow covered with parchment. The resonator is waisted on the upper side and the fingerboard is very broad. It accommodates three or four main strings, often of gut, and up to forty sympathetic strings. Because of its construction the *sarangi* is capable of great subtlety and of producing a wide range of sound. Of all north Indian instruments it most nearly reproduces the human voice

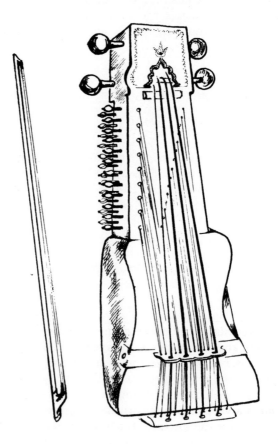

and so is the ideal accompaniment to a vocal recital. It was originally used largely for this purpose, but is now accepted as a solo instrument.

The technique of *sarangi* playing is somewhat unusual for, while the right hand wields the bow, the fingernails of the left push against and slide along the main strings.

Dilruba

The neck of a *dilruba* is much like that of a *sitar*, with domed movable frets, but its resonating chamber looks more like that of a *sarangi*, being box-like, waisted on the upper side and covered with skin. It has only one bridge which rests on the taut skin top and carries the four main strings as well as between nineteen and twenty-two sympathetic strings. It is played with a bow.

Esraj

This is a type of *sarangi* with metal strings and is used chiefly in Bengal.

Sarinda

The *sarinda* has an oval shaped resonating chamber. This is covered with wood or skin and its wider top half is open. The bridge is set on the lower half. The two strings, usually of gut, are played with a bow.

Chikara

This instrument has a rectangular resonator covered with skin. The fingerboard, which is hollow, is fretless. The three strings are either plucked or played with a bow.

Ektara

There are various types of *ektara*, meaning 'one-stringed'. Some are plucked and others are played with a bow. Allied to the *ektara* is the *dotara* which has two strings.

Veena

The *veena* is a very ancient instrument dating back, in a less developed form, to Vedic times. It is associated, traditionally, with the goddess Saraswati, the deity of learning and the fine

arts. Though more popular in Karnatic music the *veena* is also used in the North.

There are twenty-four fixed frets on a hollow wooden fingerboard which is attached to two gourds, one larger than the other. Of the seven strings, which pass over the ivory bridge, four carry the melody while the three side strings are used for rhythm and to provide the drone.

The *veena* is played either horizontally resting on the two gourds, or the smaller gourd is rested on the left knee of the seated player. Occasionally, the fingerboard slopes diagonally across the player's body so that the smaller gourd is over the left shoulder. The strings are plucked with either one or two fingers, each with a plectrum.

The *veena* is capable of producing the most delicate nuances.

Gottuvadyam

Unlike the *veena*, the *gottuvadyam* has no frets. It has four to six main strings, side strings and sympathetic strings. The strings are stopped with a cylindrical piece of horn or polished wood about an inch in diameter and two inches in length. It has a range of four to four and a half octaves and the sound produced is deeper than that of the *veena*. The *gottuvadyam* is also called the *mahanataka veena*.

Been
This is the north Indian *veena*. It has two large, equal sized, gourds which support a wooden or bamboo fingerboard. This carries the wooden frets, topped with metal, which used to be fixed but are now often movable. The strings pass over two bridges. The playing position is similar to that of the *sitar* with one gourd over the left shoulder.

Vichitra Veena
This again has two equal sized, but detachable, gourds which rest on the floor. The fretless fingerboard has four main strings and three for the drone and the rhythm. There are, in addition, eleven to thirteen sympathetic strings. The instrument is played by plucking the strings with a plectrum worn on the index finger of the right hand. The strings are stopped by sliding a glass egg up and down them with the left hand.

Tamboura
The *tamboura*, also called *tanpura*, comprises a gourd, which rests on the floor or lap, integrated with a long neck which is held upright. The function of this drone instrument is to sound the tonic constantly. There are from four to six strings and no frets. The strings are not plucked as such but are, rather, gently stroked (the Hindi word is *'chehrna'*) with the fingers of the right hand. *Tambouras* come in many sizes and pieces of quill or silk are often inserted between the strings and the bridge to create a buzzing effect.

In the Punjab and other northern regions there exists a primitive type of *tamboura* without a belly. It is merely a hollow bamboo with taut strings and, in the earthy language of the Punjab, is called *sursota*, 'drone-stick'.

Often, in the absence of a *tamboura,* the drone is provided by a harmonium, known as *sur-peti,* 'drone-box'.

Violin
The violin was introduced into India from the West over three

centuries ago, and was quickly adopted by Indian musicians. It is, however, held differently. The player sits on the floor and holds the instrument against the chest below the left shoulder. It is the most important bowed instrument in south India — an indication that the violin was probably brought in by the Portuguese.

Rabab

In shape the *rabab* is rather like the *sarod* which developed from it. Unlike the *sarod*, however, it does not have a second gourd at the top end of its broad, fretless fingerboard which is wooden. The gut strings are plucked with a horn plectrum and stopped by the fingers of the left hand. It is popular in Kashmir.

Santoor

Another instrument popular in Kashmir is the *santoor* which originated in Persia. It is a box-like instrument in the shape of a trapezium and sits in front of the player with the broad base nearest him. It has over a hundred strings which are pegged and stretched in pairs, parallel to each other. Each pair of strings passes over two bridges, one on each side of the instrument. The strings are struck by two sticks, made of walnut and curved upward at the ends.

Swarmandal

A zither-like instrument with which vocalists accompany themselves when singing. Although the *swarmandal* serves the purpose of a drone, singers occasionally play the basic melody line on the instrument.

SUSIR VADYA

Shehnai

The word *shehnai* comes from the Persian *'shah'*, 'king', and *'nai'*, 'flute'. It is, therefore, an instrument used for important occasions, both religious and secular. Traditionally it is associated with weddings. A double reeded flute, the *shehnai's* seven, eight, or nine holes are on the staff and stopped by the fingers. The last two holes are used for tuning and are either

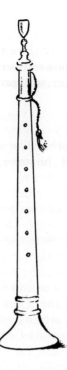

left open or stopped with wax. The drone accompaniment of a *shehnai* is always another *shehnai*. Strong breath control is needed to play this instrument, particularly for long sustained passages which can be in an incredibly fast tempo.

The *shehnai's* nearest Western equivalent is the oboe.

Nadaswaram

This is the *shehnai's* sister instrument in south India. Much larger than the *shehnai*, sometimes made of silver but more often of wood, the *nadaswaram* has twelve holes, six of which are for playing and six to regulate pitch.

The *ninkirna* is a smaller type of *nadaswaram*. The *pongi* is another type which is used to give the drone accompaniment during a *nadaswaram* recital.

Bansari

This word covers a variety of flutes. *'Banse'* means 'bamboo', and so any flute made of bamboo is called a *bansari*. Nowadays, of course, many are made of metal. A number are end-blown while others, like the god Krishna's *murli*, are side-blown.

The humble *bansari* with its range of just under two octaves has been developed and elevated to the concert platform. Also long modern flutes, with a wider range, are now being made to meet the special demands of classical music.

Other Wind Instruments

Among these are the *venu*, a south Indian side flute with one end stopped and eight finger holes; the *kuma*, or brass trumpet; the *tota*, a small flute used in north India; the *panji*, with a small gourd, much used by snake-charmers; the *nallatarang*, a type of organ; the *kural*, or panpipe; the *nausbaga*, or bagpipe; the *karana*, or wooden trumpet; various kinds of horns, many of them buffalo horns, known as *turafu*; and, in a special category, the *shank*, or conch shell, so important in Hindu religious ritual.

AVANADA VADYA

Tabla

The full name of this instrument is *tabla-bañya* and it consists of two drums — the *tabla* being the right hand drum and the *bañya*, also known as the *dugga*, the left. Both drum heads are of skin with a paste of iron filings and flour in the centre, but the body of the *bañya*, the bass drum, is metal, and that of the *tabla* wood. The *tabla* is usually tuned to the tonic, dominant or subdominant of the *raga*. This is done by knocking the blocks, which are held by braces on the sides of the instrument, into place. Sometimes the re-tuning has to be done during a performance because the heat of the lights often alters the setting. The *tabla* has a range of about one octave.

First used in India during the Muslim period, the *tabla* is today the most popular of all the many kinds of drums in north India.

Pakhavaj

An older form of drum than the *tabla*, the *pakhavaj* is about two and a half feet long and was originally made of clay but now more often of wood. It has two parchment heads, each tuned to a different pitch. Like the *tabla*, the tuning is done by knocking the side blocks into place. A paste of boiled rice, manganese dust or iron filings and tamarind juice is applied to the smaller head; and a wheat flour paste on the larger head helps to produce the lower notes. These paste centres, unlike those of the *tabla*, have to be removed after each performance and put on afresh for the next.

The *pakhavaj* has a deep, mellow sound and is used to accompany *dhrupad* and *dhamar* singing and the music of the *been* and *rabab*. Ideally, it is also used to accompany *Kathak* dancing. The *pakhavaj* is often known as the *mridang*.

Mridangam

The *mridangam* is as widely used in the South as the *tabla* is in the North. It is like the *pakhavaj* but somewhat smaller and thinner, and is now made more often of wood than clay. The bass left head is covered with two layers of skin and has a centre of boiled rice, manganese filings and water. The head played with the right hand is smaller and is covered with three different skins. This too has a centre of paste which is permanent and is tuned to SA. The tuning is done in the same way as that of the *pakhavaj*.

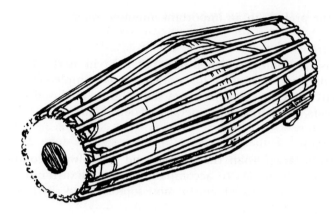

In the hands of a master, the *mridangam* is capable of producing quite as much subtlety and excitement as the *tabla* and deserves to be better known in the West.

Chenda
This is a cylindrical drum which is held upright and struck with two slender sticks. It has a very penetrating sound which carries over long distances. Used mainly in Kerala, in south-west India, the *chenda* announces the start of the *Kathakali* dance dramas. During the performance itself it creates many sound effects — from the gentle patter of rain to the roar of thunder.

Dholak
A drum made from hollowed out wood, fat waisted and tapering towards the ends. The two drum heads are of skin stretched over hoops. The pitch is varied by adjusting the rings through which pass the interlacing cords that link the drum heads. The *dholak* is popular as an accompaniment to folk music in north India. It is played with the fingers and usually a second person keeps time with a ring or small stone on the body of the drum.

Dhol
A large drum played with a pair of sticks. It is loud and lacks subtlety. The *dhol* is used in tribal and rural areas, very often

as the prelude to an important announcement.

Gharha
This is a porous earthenware pot used in north India for keeping water cool or for storage. It is completely circular apart from the short neck and slight lip. It is played with the fingers, sometimes with metal rings on them.

Ghatam
This is larger than the *gharha* and not always completely circular. It is used to accompany south Indian music. Some *ghatam* players produce the most sophisticated rhythms.

Kanjira
A small tambourine-like instrument with copper or bronze discs on the frame. It has only one skin of goat or lizard. It is held in the left hand and struck with the fingers and palm of the right.

Duff
This is a much bigger version of the *kanjira* and is struck either with the hand or a stick.

Damru
A small hour-glass shaped drum, to the waist of which is attached a leather thong. The *damru* is held in one hand and shaken so that the weighted thong strikes the two parchment or vellum heads which are stretched over hoops and tightened with cords.

A larger drum, similar in shape to the *damru*, is the *udukku* of south India.

Other Drums
Some of the other drums of India are the *nal* of Maharashtra; the *maddallam* of Kerala; the *khol* of Bengal; the *pung* of Manipur; and the *madal* of the tribal peoples of Bihar. Among the kettledrums are the *tasha* which is high pitched and the *nakkara* or *nagara*, used for ceremonial occasions and sometimes slung in pairs on elephants and horses. A larger kettledrum is the *karadsamila*, conical in shape. All over south

India the barrel-shaped *tavil* accompanies the *nadaswaram* and Kerala, in particular, has the medium sized hour-glass shaped *timila*.

GHANA VADYA

There are many types of temple bells and gongs. Among the cymbals are the small brass, dome-shaped, *manjira,* and the larger *jhanj* and *kartal.* The *kash-tarang* is a xylophone made of wood and is played with a pair of sticks.

The *jaltarang* is the best known name under this heading. It consists of a series of porcelain bowls of different sizes, each containing a particular volume of water. The bowls are struck with a pair of small sticks so that the instrument is rather like a water xylophone. Sometimes the sticks are discarded and the player rubs the rims of the bowls with a wet finger. The *jaltarang,* in such instances, becomes a glass harmonica.

15   The Musicians

In this chapter are listed the names of musicians of merit, both living and of the recent past. The list is, however, by no means comprehensive for a number of musicians had to be excluded by reason of the paucity of information available about them. The names of the artists are given in the form by which they are best known. Honorifics such as "Pandit" and "Ustad" have, by and large, not been used.

ABDUL HALIM JAFFER KHAN Hindustani (*sitar*)
Son of Jaffer Khan of the Indore *gharana*, Abdul Halim Jaffer Khan is a respected instrumentalist. He is based in Bombay.

ABDUL KARIM KHAN Hindustani (vocalist)
Abdul Karim Khan, who died in 1937, belonged to the Kirana *gharana*. He trained with Kalé Khan and Abdulla Khan and, apart from voice culture, learnt the *veena* and the *sarangi*. His first appointment was at the Baroda court but it was at Miraj that he finally settled. In 1913 he founded the Arya Sangeet Vidyalaya in Poona. His interests and sympathies were very wide for he made a serious study of the Karnatic *ragas* and introduced them into his programmes.

One of Abdul Karim Kahn's best known pupils was Rambhau Kundgolkar, also called 'Sawai Gandharva'.

AHMEDJAN 'THIRAKWA' Hindustani (*tabla*)
The son of Hussein Bux Khan, Ahmedjan was born at Moradabad in 1891. He studied with Munir Khan, Sher Khan and Faiyaz Khan. Later, he acquired the cognomen 'Thirakwa'

as an onomatopoeic description of his *tabla* playing. In 1954 he was honoured as the doyen of *tabla* players when he received the Sangeet Natak Akademi award. He was professor of *tabla* at the Bhatkhande Music College at Lucknow.

AHMED REZA KHAN Hindustani (*vichitra veena*)
Ahmed Reza Khan hails from a family of musicians originally from Moradabad, Uttar Pradesh. He trained under Abdul Aziz Khan and is now on the staff of All India Radio, Delhi.

ALI AKBAR KHAN Hindustani (*sarod*, also composer)
Born in 1922 at Shibpore in what is now Bangladesh, Ali Akbar learnt the *sarod* from his father Allauddin Khan. Later, under his uncle Aftabuddin, he studied the *tabla* and the *pakhavaj*. He has toured the world many times and has appeared at various international music festivals.

Ali Akbar has composed some new *ragas* and has made many recordings. In 1956 he founded the Ali Akbar College of Music at Calcutta and many of his students, which include his son Ashish Khan, have attained international stature. He has composed for films, the best known of which is *Hungry Stones*.

In 1963 he received a Sangeet Natak Akademi award.

ALLA RAKHA Hindustani (*tabla*, also composer)
Alla Rakha was born in 1919 and trained with Kadir Baksh of the Punjab *gharana*. He has provided the music for many films under the name of A.R. Qureshi. For many years he toured widely with Ravi Shankar. Many of Alla Rakha's pupils have become *tabla* players of the highest class.

ALLAUDDIN KHAN Hindustani (*sarod*, also composer)
Widely regarded as the Grand Old Man of Hindustani music, Allauddin Khan died in 1972 aged over a hundred. He was born at Shibpore and studied with Gopal Chandra Chatterjee, Lobo, Munne Khan and Ahmed Ali Khan. He finally managed, after many struggles, to become the *shahgird* of Mohammad Vazir Khan of Rampur. In 1935 he toured Europe with Uday Shankar's company. In 1952 he was honoured by the Sangeet Natak Akademi and in 1958 was made a Padma Bhushan by the Indian government.

A prolific composer, Allauddin Khan composed many *ragas* that are now well known and founded a *gharana* which is named after him. His best known pupils are Ravi Shankar, who became his son-in-law, Ali Akbar Khan, his son, and Annapurna, his daughter.

AMAN ALI KHAN 'AMAR' Hindustani (vocalist, also composer)
Aman Ali Khan represented the Gwalior *gharana*. He was a gifted singer, composer and teacher. Many of his compositions were a skilful synthesis of the Hindustani and Karnatic styles. He was the son of Chajju Khan, whose pen-name was also 'Amar'.

AMBALAPUZHA BROTHERS Karnatic (*nadaswaram*)
K. Sankaranarayana Panicker and K. Gopalakrishna Panicker, named 'Ambalapuzha' after their birthplace, studied with P.S. Veeruswamy Pillai. They made numerous recordings and had a large and faithful following.

AMIR KHAN Hindustani (vocalist)
Born in 1912, Amir Khan studied with Shammir Khan and specialized in the *khayal* singing of the Indore *gharana*. He was a Fellow of the Bihar Akademi and holder of the 1967 Sangeet Natak Akademi award. He did much research on the *tarana* and the *khayal*.

AMJAD ALI KHAN Hindustani (*sarod*)
Born in 1945, Amjad Ali Khan studied under his father Hafiz Ali Khan of Gwalior. He has a worldwide following for he has given to the *sarod* a new and exciting dimension. He has been awarded several titles and honours and is the first north Indian musician to have performed in honour of Thyagaraja at the saint-musicians's Thiruvaiyar shrine. In 1981 he performed in Pakistan thus breaking a long cultural silence between India and Pakistan. He is the founder of the Ustad Hazif Ali Khan Memorial Society, in honour of his father, which organizes music festivals in different parts of India.

ARIYAKKUDI RAMANUJA IYENGAR Karnatic (vocalist)
A disciple of Pudukkotai Iyer, Narasimha Iyengar and

Srinivasa Iyengar, Ariyakkudi Ramanuja Iyengar was a specialist in *bhajans* and *kirtis*. He regularly led the devotional singing at the shrine of Thyagaraja, the saint musician. He was also a popular exponent of light *ragas*.

ASAD ALI KHAN Hindustani (*been*)
An outstanding instrumentalist of the Khandar *bani* style, Asad Ali Khan's forebears were musicians at the courts of Rampur, Jaipur and Alwar. In 1977 he was honoured with a Sangeet Natak Akademi award. Asad Ali Khan also performs on a version of the *been* called the *rudra veena*.

ASUTOSH BHATTACHARYA Folk Music (musicologist)
Dr. Bhattacharya, director of the Research Institute of Folk Culture in Calcutta, has done much to preserve and record the folk music of Bengal. In 1966 he was made a Fellow of the Sangeet Natak Akademi.

BADÉ GHULAM ALI KHAN Hindustani (vocalist)
Born in 1901 in Lahore, now in Pakistan, Badé Ghulam Ali Khan belonged to the Patiala *gharana*. He learnt from his father, Khan Sahib Ali Bux, and his uncle, Kalé Khan. Later he studied with Wahid Khan, Baba Sindhi Khan, and Ashiq Ali of Patiala. Badé Ghulam Ali Khan's forte was light classical music, particularly *thumris*. Many of these he composed himself under the pen-name 'Sabrang'.

His chief pupil was his son, Munawar Ali Khan, who died recently. His grandson Raza Ali Khan is a noted singer.

BAHADUR KHAN Hindustani (*sarod*)
One of the distinguished pupils of the late Allauddin Khan, Bahadur Khan was born in 1929. He has made many disc recordings and has toured China, the Middle East and the former U.S.S.R.

BALACHANDER Karnatic (*veena*)
Among the major musicians of India, S. Balachander was probably unique not because he was a child prodigy but because he was self-taught. Born in 1927, he learnt to play the *kanjira* when he was very young and soon started appearing in concert

performances. By the time he was fifteen he had learnt to play several instruments so competently that he was able to join the staff of All India Radio, Madras. Later, he became an established *veena* artist. His interests ranged over Hindustani as well as Western music.

Balachander composed for films and his records are still very popular. He toured abroad several times.

BALASARASWATI Karnatic (vocalist, also dancer)
T. Balasaraswati was known to the world primarily as a great *Bharata Natyam* dancer. However, her singing, particularly of *padams*, was of the highest quality. Her mother, Jayammal, and her grandmother, Veena Dhanam, were celebrated musicians.

Balasaraswati toured the world several times and was honoured by the Sangeet Natak Akademi in 1955. In 1957 the Indian government gave her the Padma Bhushan. Her daughter Lakshmi teaches in the U.S.A.

BALKRISHNA RAGHUNATH DEODHAR Hindustani (vocalist, also musicologist)
Born in 1902, Prof. Deodhar was a respected name in Indian music. He studied with V. D. Paluskar and Shende Khan and sang *khayal* of the Gwalior *gharana*. In 1925 he founded the School of Indian Music in Bombay and held many academic posts. A member of the executive board of the Sangeet Natak Akademi, he attended international music conferences and researched voice culture.

BALWANT RAI VERMA Hindustani (*sitar*)
Balwant Rai Verma, born in 1930, studied with Ravi Shankar and now teaches at Delhi University.

BARKAT ALI KHAN Pakistani (vocalist)
Barkat Ali Khan was the younger brother of Badé Ghulam Ali Khan. He was born at Kasur in the Punjab and learnt from his father and elder brother. He developed his own style of *ghazal*, *thumri* and *dadra* singing. His death in 1963 robbed Pakistan of an artist of the highest rank.

BEGUM AKHTAR Hindustani (vocalist)
After having studied with Atta Ahmed Khan of the Patiala

gharana, Begum Akhtar became a famous singer of *ghazals*, *thumris*, *bhajans* and *dadras*. Her many records are still popular all over the subcontinent.

BHAI LAL Pakistani (vocalist)
Born at Amritsar, Bhai Lal studied *khayal* with Bhaskar Rao. He wrote on musical subjects and was music adviser to Radio Pakistan. His son Ghulam Hussain Shagan is a *khayal* singer of merit.

BHIMSEN JOSHI Hindustani (vocalist)
Bhimsen Joshi, born in 1922, is a popular and outstanding *khayal* singer of the Kirana *gharana*. His teacher was Rambhau Kundgolkar. He has made a large number of records.

BHOODALUR S. KRISHNAMOORTHY SASTRY Karnatic (*gottuvadyam*, also vocalist)
A well known teacher of music, Krishnamoorthy Sastry was principal of the Kalakshetra academy at Tiruvanmiyur, Madras. Among his honours is a Sangeet Natak Akademi award. He trained with K. Vidyanatha Iyer and Muthaiah Bhagavatar.

BIGAMUDRE CHAITANYA DEVA Hindustani (vocalist, also musicologist)
Dr. Deva, born in 1922, worked for the Sangeet Natak Akademi as special officer for music. Trained in the *khayal* of the Gwalior and Bhendi Bazar *gharanas*, he studied the psychoacoustics of music and speech and the tonal structure of the *tamboura*.

BIRENDRA KISHORE ROY CHOUDHURY Hindustani (vocalist, also musicologist)
Born in 1903, B.K. Roy Choudhury studied with Mohammad Dabir Khan, Ali Khan and Sagir Khan. He sang in the *dhrupad* style and also played the *been* and *rabab*. His research work centred mainly on the *dhrupad*.

A Fellow of the Sangeet Natak Akademi, his chief publications were *Indian Music and Miaṅ Tansen* and *Raga Sangeet*.

BISMILLAH KHAN Hindustani (*shehnai*)
Bismillah Khan, born in 1916, is the son of Paigambar Bux who was employed as a musician by the ruler of Dumraon. He trained with his uncle Ali Bux and appeared with him at music conferences. In 1940 — after Ali Bux's death — he became an artist in his own right. Bismillah Khan's dislike of air travel has kept him away from the international scene. However, he appeared at the Edinburgh Festival and the Commonwealth Arts Festival in 1965. Two years later he performed at Expo '67 in Montreal. In 1993 he played in London.

Bismillah Khan has made a large number of records. He received the Sangeet Natak Akademi award in 1956, the Padma Shri in 1961 and the Padma Bhushan in 1968.

CHITTI BABU Karnatic (*veena*)
Chitti Babu, born in 1936, studied with Emani Sankara Sastry and is a fine *veena* player. He has made many records. In 1968 he toured Europe.

CHITTOOR SUBRAMANIAM Karnatic (vocalist)
A well known teacher, Chittoor Subramaniam was head of the music department of Annamalai University. He was honoured by the Madras Music Academy and the Sangeet Natak Akademi.

DAGAR BROTHERS Hindustani (vocalists)
Aminuddin Khan Dagar is descended from a long line of famous *dhrupad* singers. The family includes such illustrious artists as Nasiruddin Khan Dagar, Riazuddin Khan Dagar, Ziauddin Khan Dagar, Rahimuddin Khan Dagar, Zakiruddin Khan Dagar, Rahim Fahimuddin Khan Dagar, Imamuddin Khan Dagar and Hasinuddin Khan Dagar. Aminuddin Khan Dagar and his late brother Moinuddin Khan Dagar toured abroad extensively. The two Nandy sisters are their chief pupils.

DEBABRATA CHAUDHURI Hindustani (*sitar*)
Debabrata Chaudhuri was born in 1935 in Calcutta where he became the pupil of Mushtaq Ali Khan of the Seniya *gharana*. Since his first appearance in London in 1968 he has toured in

almost every part of the world and has played at many festivals. He teaches at Delhi University and at the Bharatiya Kala Kendra.

DILIP CHANDRA VEDI Hindustani (vocalist)
Professor of vocal music at the Bharatiya Kala Kendra, New Delhi, Dilip Chandra Vedi sings both *khayal* and *dhrupad*. He trained with Bhaskar Rao Bakhle, Faiyaz Khan, Alladiya Khan, Hyder Bux and Uttam Singh. He has done much research and has made many recordings.

DILIP KUMAR ROY Hindustani (vocalist)
D.K. Roy learnt from teachers such as Abdul Karim Khan, Faiyaz Khan and V.N. Bhatkhande. He toured abroad many times and made numerous recordings. In 1965 he was elected to the Sankeet Natak Akademi. In later life Roy became a *sanyasi*.

DILSHAD KHAN and PARVEEN SULTANA Hindustani (vocalists)
Dilshad Khan studied under Jnan Prakash Ghosh, N.C. Chakraborty, N. Banerjee, Fayaz Ahmed and Niaz Ahmed and had as his mentor Badé Ghulam Ali Khan. Later he researched music under Dr. Bimal Roy. His wife Parveen Sultana first studied under her father Ikramul Majid and then under Chinmoy Lahiri. This duo has made a mark on the international music scene.

DWARAM VENKATASWAMY NAIDU Karnatic (violin)
Venkataswamy Naidu studied the violin from an early age, his teachers being Sangameswara Sastri, Tirukodikavil Krishna Iyer, Venkanna Pantulu and Govindaswamy Pillay. At thirteen he made his first successful public appearance and at twenty-six became professor of violin at the Vizianagaram Music College. In 1950 he was awarded an honorary doctorate by Andhra University and three years later received the President's award for Karnatic music.

   He studied Western techniques of violin playing and adjusted his own to good effect. He often played Hindustani music as well as Mendelssohn, Bach and Rossini.

FAIYAZ KHAN Hindustani (vocalist)
Faiyaz Khan was from an illustrious family of musicians, his great-grandfather being the famous 'Rangila' Ramzan Khan. The *gharana*, therefore, was known as Rangila *gharana*. Faiyaz Khan learnt from his grandfather, Ghulam Abbas Khan, and Kallan Khan. He began his professional career at eighteen. While he was still young the celebrated Miyanjan Khan acknowledged him as a master. In 1908, Faiyaz Khan sang in competition with Hafiz Khan, the Maharaja of Mysore's court musician, and the prize money had to be divided equally between them. It was then that the ruler gave Faiyaz Khan the title of *Aftab-ê-Mausiqi*, 'The Sun of Music'.

Faiyaz Khan's repertoire ranged from *dhrupad* to *thumri* and *ghazal* and he composed under the pen-name 'Prem Piya'. He became a musician at the Baroda court and helped his friend Bhatkhande with the *Kramik Pustak* series.

FAIYAZ KHAN Hindustani (*tabla*)
Born in 1935 in Jaipur, Faiyaz Khan began his musical training as a singer and *sarangi* player but later changed to the *tabla*. His teachers were his father Nazir Khan, Hidayat Khan, Inam Ali Khan and Ramnad Ishwaran. He is on the staff of All India Radio and has toured abroad several times.

FATEH ALI KHAN Pakistani (vocalist)
Fateh Ali Khan is a noted *khayal* singer of the Patiala *gharana*. He learnt from his father Akhtar Hussain Khan who was the son of the famous Ali Baksh Khan. Fateh Ali Khan is a master of technique and *taans*. His elder brother Amanat Ali Khan, who died in 1974, was a master of melody.

FEROZE NIZAMI Pakistani (vocalist, also musicologist)
Born in Lahore in 1916, Feroze Nizami belonged to the Kirana *gharana* and studied with Abdul Wahid Khan. He composed for films and wrote widely on music. He was professor of music with the Pakistan Arts Council in Lahore.

GANGUBAI HANGAL Hindustani (vocalist)
A distinguished singer of the Kirana *gharana*. Gangubai Hangal studied with Rambhau Kundgolkar. She has toured

the neighbouring countries of India and has made a few recordings.

GIRIJA DEVI Hindustani (vocalist)
Girija Devi was born in 1929 and trained with Sarju Prasad Misra and Sri Chandra Misra. She is a well known exponent of the vocal style of the Seniya *gharana* and has made a number of records. She toured Europe in 1970.

GURDEV SINGH Hindustani (*sarod*)
Born in 1948, the London-based Gurdev Singh is an outstanding pupil of Amjad Ali Khan. He also plays the *dilruba* and is a trained vocalist. Gurdev Singh has performed in several countries with distinction and has many students in England.

HAFIZ ALI KHAN Hindustani (*sarod*)
Hazif Ali Khan studied the *sarod* with his father Nanne Khan and *dhrupad* with Ganeshlal Chaubey and Vazir Khan. He was court musician at Gwalior and later became professor of instrumental music at the Bharatiya Kala Kendra, New Delhi. In 1953 he received the Sangeet Natak Akademi award and became a Fellow of the academy in the following year. In 1960 he was made a Padma Bhushan.

HARI PRASAD CHAURASIA Hindustani (flute)
Born in 1938, Hari Prasad Chaurasia is a Bachelor of Music and trained as a singer with Annapurna Shankar. He then learnt the flute from Raja Ram and continued his studies with Bhola Nath. For a time he worked with All India Radio. He is equally at home in the popular music of films, in folk music and on the concert platform with classical music.

HIRABAI BARODEKAR Hindustani (vocalist)
Born in 1905 at Miraj, Hirabai Barodekar studied with Vahid Khan and her brother Suresh Mané, a pupil of Abdul Karim Khan. Her first public performance was at the age of fifteen when she appeared under the patronage of Kesarbai Kerkar. She encouraged women to study music and pioneered the introduction of classical music to the Marathi stage.

Hirabai Barodekar and her brother started a music school in Bombay which was very successful.

IMRAT KHAN Hindustani (*surbahar*)
Imrat Khan, born in 1935, learnt the *surbahar* from his uncle Vahid Khan and the *sitar* from his brother Vilayat Khan. Vocal music was the speciality of his mother's family and this he learnt from his maternal grandfather Bandé Hassan Khan. He has been on numerous concert tours abroad and has performed at major festivals. Imrat Khan was the first Indian musician to perform at the Henry Wood Promenade Concerts in London. His sons Nishat and Wajahat are now established musicians.

IRENE ROY CHOUDHURI Hindustani (vocalist)
After study with the Dagar Brothers, Irene Roy Choudhuri took a great interest in *Rabindra-sangeet*. A staff artist with All India Radio, she has toured Britain, the former U.S.S.R., and several countries of the East.

JAYACHAMARAJA WADIYAR Karnatic (musicologist)
Jayachamaraja Wadiyar, although trained in Western music, composed many *kritis*. His interests ranged from philosophy to the preservation of wild life. He published many books and lectured abroad extensively.

Dr. Wadiyar was the last Maharaja of Mysore and from 1961 to 1965 was the chairman of the Sangeet Natak Akademi.

JNAN PRAKASH GHOSH Hindustani (vocalist)
After studying with many distinguished teachers such as Maseet Khan, Dabir Khan and Shankar Chakravarti, Jnan Prakash Ghosh became an All India Radio producer. As a *khayal* singer he is much in demand. In 1954 he toured Europe.

KADIR BAKSH Pakistani (*tabla*)
An exponent of the Punjab *gharana*, Kadir Baksh was a famous *tabla* and *pakhavaj* player. Before Partition his fellow musicians awarded him with the title of Rustam-é-Hind of *tabla* playing, for he had a particularly powerful style. He learnt from his father Fakir Baksh who was a musician with the Maharaja of Kashmir. Kadir Baksh wrote many compositions for the *tabla*.

Alla Rakha, of India, and Alla Ditta, of Pakistan, are two of his best known pupils.

KAILAS CHANDRA DEVA BRAHASPATI Hindustani (vocalist, also musicologist)
A scholar of wide learning and musical experience, Dr. Brahaspati, born in 1918, trained with Ayodhya Prasad and Mirza Nawab Hussein. He did much research and designed new instruments. His books, *Sangeet Chintamani* and *Bharat ka Sangeet Siddhant*, are well known. He was chief music adviser to All India Radio.

KANAI DATTA Hindustani (*tabla*)
Born in 1924, Kanai Datta is a leading *tabla* artist. He trained with Jnan Prakash Ghosh. He has toured Europe and north America.

KANTHE MAHARAJ Hindustani (*tabla*)
Kanthe Maharaj was a famous *tabla* player some years ago. A member of the Varanasi *gharana*, Kanthe Maharaj made many recordings and received a Sangeet Natak Akademi award in 1961.

KESARBAI KERKAR Hindustani (vocalist)
Kesarbai Kerkar was born in 1892 and studied with Alladiya Khan. She specialized in the *khayal* of the Jaipur *gharana*. She was a Padma Shri and received a Sangeet Natak Akademi award in 1953.

KISHAN MAHARAJ Hindustani (*tabla*)
Kishan Maharaj was born in 1923 in Varanasi and studied with Kanthe Maharaj. He has accompanied some of the finest musicians and toured Europe in 1954. In 1965 he performed at the Commonwealth Arts Festival in London.

KUMBHAKONAM RAJAMANICKAM PILLAI Karnatic (violin)
Rajamanickam Pillai was a musician to the Maharaja of Travancore. His teacher was T. Ramaswami Iyer. He was honoured by the Sangeet Natak Akademi and the Madras Music Academy.

LAKSHMI SHANKAR Hindustani (vocalist)
Lakshmi Shankar trained under B.R. Deodhar, Ravi Shankar
and Abdul Rehman Khan. She sings in the *khayal* style of the
Patiala *gharana*. However, she has also studied Karnatic music.
Her numerous recordings are in constant demand and she has
made many tours abroad.

LAL MANI MISRA Hindustani (*vichitra veena* and *sitar*)
Dr. Misra is reader in music at Benares Hindu University. He
studied with Mehndi Hussein Khan, Swami Pramodanand,
Sukhdev Rai and Abdul Aziz Khan. His chief publication is
Sangeet Sarita. He has toured Europe and America.

LALGUDI JAYARAMAN Karnatic (violin)
Born in 1930, Lalgudi Jayaraman trained with Lalgudi V.R.
Gopala Iyer and is a highly gifted and well known
instrumentalist. In 1965 he represented India at the
Commonwealth Arts Festival in London.

LATIF AHMED KHAN Hindustani (*tabla*)
Latif Ahmed Khan, born in 1942, trained with Gamé Khan,
Inam Ali Khan, and Munnu Khan. His style, therefore, was that
of the Delhi *gharana*. He toured abroad several times.

LOBO, ANTSHER Hindustani (vocalist, also musicologist)
Born in 1905, Antsher Lobo sang *khayal* in the style of the
Jaipur *gharana*. He studied with Alladiya Khan. His knowledge
of Western music imparted an extra dimension to his work as a
musicologist. He made a few recordings.

M.S. GOPALAKRISHNAN Karnatic (violin)
M.S. Gopalakrishnan was born in 1931. His father and elder
brother were both professional violinists. After training with
his father, he accompanied Omkarnath Thakur on several
occasions. Thus Gopalakrishnan learnt Hindustani music as
well. His interests extend to Western music, particularly where
the violin is concerned.

MADURAI MANI IYER Karnatic (vocalist)
Born in 1912, Mani Iyer trained with Harikesanallur Muthaiah

and Rajan Bhagavatar. He has made many disc recordings and has been honoured by the Madras Music Academy and the Sangeet Natak Academi.

MAHALINGAM RAMASWAMY IYER Karnatic (flute)
A child prodigy, Ramaswamy Iyer was first trained by his uncle Rajagopala Iyer. Later, however, he perfected his own original style. He has published a manual on flute playing and received an award from the Sangeet Natak Akademi in 1965.

MAHAPURUSH MISRA Hindustani (*tabla*)
Born in 1933, Mahapurush Misra studied with Swaran Paramhansa, Ganesh Paramhans and Anokhe Lal. He has made a number of recordings and has toured Europe, America and Japan.

MANIK RAO POPATKAR Hindustani (*tabla*)
A well known player of the Varanasi *gharana*, Manik Rao Popatkar trained with Samta Prasad. He has toured abroad.

MANILAL NAG Hindustani (*sitar*)
Manilal Nag is a leading musician of the Vishnupur *gharana* of Bengal. He studied under his father Gokhul Nag who was a disciple of Ram Prasanna Bannerjee.

MATHOOR SHANKARAMURTI Karnatic (musicologist)
After rigorous training under Rama Jois, Chambai Vaidyanatha Bhagavatar, Keshava Murthy and Sattur Krishna Iyengar, Mathoor Shankaramurti became a researcher and teacher. His *Karnataka Sangeetha Tarangini* series, which consists of over 50 volumes, is a landmark of Karnatic music research. He researched the influence of European music on Dikshitar and Thyagaraja. He died in 1993.

MOHAMMAD DABIR KHAN Hindustani (*been*, also vocalist)
This descendant of Tansen was also known as Dayal Singh, which was his Hindu name. He was born in 1907 and trained under his grandfather Mohammad Vazir Khan who was at the Rampur court. His singing was strictly in the *dhrupad* style. He was, for many years, the head of the Tansen Music College in Calcutta.

MOKKAPATI NAGESWARA RAO Karnatic (*veena*)
Nageswara Rao, who was born in 1926, studied with Behta Rajarao, Kalyanakrishna Bhagavatar, Sivanandam and Narayana Iyengar. He is an important *veena* artist and has made many recordings. Nageswara Rao has worked with Maurice Bejart and has toured abroad many times.

MRINAL SEN GUPTA Hindustani (*sarod*)
After starting as a flutist, Mrinal Sen Gupta chose the *sarod* as his instrument. He studied with Ali Akbar Khan and, on completing his training, worked for the Bharatiya Kala Kendra and the Triveni Kala Sangam. He has toured abroad.

MUDICONDAN C. VENKATARAMA IYER Karnatic (vocalist)
After studying with a number of teachers, Venkatarama Iyer became a well known singer. He has written on Karnatic music and has been honoured by the Sangeet Natak Akademi and the Madras Music Academy. He heads the music department of a teachers' training college in Madras.

MUSIRI SUBRAMANIA IYER Karnatic (vocalist)
Musiri Subramania Iyer, an academic of high distinction, was at the Travancore court. His teachers were N.N. Iyengar, K.C. Iyer and S. Iyer. Later he became principal of the College of Music, Annamalai University. In 1968 he became a Fellow of the Sangeet Natak Akademi.

N. RAMANI Karnatic (flute)
Born in 1934, N. Ramani studied with Mahalingam Ramaswamy Iyer. He is today one of the important flutists of south India.

NARAYANA MENON, V.K. Karnatic (*veena*, also musicologist)
Dr. Menon was born in 1911 and, apart from his music, was an artistic administrator. He has been director-general of All India Radio, secretary of the Sangeet Natak Akademi, and president of the International Music Council. He was director of the Institute of Performing Arts in Bombay.

Dr. Menon has specialized in comparative musicology and has been on many lecture and concert tours abroad.

NIKHIL BANERJEE Hindustani (*sitar*)
The son of Jitendra Nath Banerjee, a well known *sitar* player, Nikhil Banerjee was born in 1931 in Calcutta. He was first taught by his father and then by Allauddin Khan and Ali Akbar Khan. He made many recordings and toured abroad extensively. In 1967 he was awarded the Padma Shri. A distinguished artist, Nikhil Banerjee was widely respected in Indian music circles.

NIKHIL JYOTI GHOSH Hindustani
(*tabla*, also vocalist and musicologist)
Nikhil Ghosh was born on New Year's day, 1919. His teachers were Amir Hussein Khan, Bipin Chatterjee, Feroze Nizami, Jnan Prakash Ghosh, Ahmedjan 'Thirakwa', and his brother Pannalal Ghosh. He is principal of the Sangeet Mahabharati, Bombay, and published *Fundamentals of Raga and Tala: with a new system of notation* in 1968. Nikhil Ghosh is very interested in improving and modernising musical training in India. He heads an academic board that is compiling an encyclopaedia of Indian music. In 1974 he toured Europe and America.

OMKARNATH THAKUR Hindustani (vocalist, also musicologist)
Pandit Omkarnath Thakur, who died in 1967, was one of the leading singers of his day. After a difficult childhood he managed to get to Bombay where he became the pupil of V.D. Paluskar. Later, he was appointed principal of the Gandharva Mahavidyalaya at Lahore. After Partition he came to Delhi. He toured abroad many times, made several recordings and wrote a number of books on the theory and practice of music.

P.S. VEERUSWAMY PILLAI Karnatic (*nadaswaram*)
One of the foremost names associated with the *nadaswaram*, Veeruswarmy Pillai was a temple musician for many years. He was honoured by the Sangeet Natak Akademi in 1966.

P.V. RAJAMANNAR Karnatic (musicologist)
Dr. Rajamannar is critic, author and artistic administrator. A former chief justice of the Madras High Court, he was the first chairman of the Sangeet Natak Akademi, from 1953 to 1961.

PALGHAT K.V. NARAYANASWAMY Karnatic (vocalist)
K.V. Narayanaswamy was born in 1923 and studied with
Ariyakkudi Ramanuja Iyengar. He has taught at the Central
College of Karnatic Music in Madras and in the U.S.A. In 1965
he sang at the Commonwealth Arts Festival in London.

PALGHAT MANI IYER Karnatic (*mridangam*)
Born in 1913, Mani Iyer began playing the *mridangam* at an
early age. His *gurus* were C. Subba Iyer and T.V. Iyer. By the
age of fourteen he had become a brilliant percussionist. For a
time he was employed by the Maharaja of Travancore. He was
honoured by the Madras Music Academy and the Sangeet
Natak Akademi (1956).
　　Palghat Mani Iyer performed at the Edinburgh Festival and
the Commonwealth Arts Festival in 1965.

PANNALAL GHOSH Hindustani (flute)
Born in 1911 in the Barisal district of what is now Bangladesh,
Pannalal Ghosh taught himself to play the simple country flute
while he was still a young boy. Most of his time, however, was
spent in activities such as wrestling, fencing and boxing. In
1936 he won a boxing championship and for a time worked in a
circus. He then joined the film industry as a musician and
became the pupil of Khushi Mohammad. He then studied with
Shankar Chakravarti. Later he persuaded Allauddin Khan to
coach him.
　　In time Pannalal Ghosh became the leading flute player in
India. He devised for himself flutes which were sometimes over
a yard long and did much to have the flute accepted as a concert
instrument. He died in 1960.

PREM LATA SHARMA Hindustani (vocalist, also musicologist)
Dr. Sharma, born in 1927, was trained by Omkarnath Thakur.
She heads the department of musicology at Benares Hindu
University. In 1966 she represented India at the Moscow
Conservatoire's centenary celebrations. Her research has been
mainly concerned with the history and aesthetics of Indian
music.

PROFESSOR P. SAMBAMOORTHY Karnatic (musicologist)
Prof. Sambamoorthy, an honoured name in Karnatic music, was formerly head of the music department of Madras University. A Fellow of the Sangeet Natak Akademi, he has represented India at various international music conferences. He is a composer and has made many recordings. His *South Indian Music Book*, in five volumes, is a comprehensive work.

RADHIKA MOHAN MAITRA Hindustani (*sarod*, also *sitar*)
Born in 1917, Radhika Mohan Maitra studied with Amir Khan and Mohammad Dabir Khan. He has made many recordings and toured China in 1955.

RAIS KHAN Hindustani (*sitar*)
A captivating musician, Rais Khan belongs to the Indore *gharana*. He lives in Bombay and is related, through his mother, to Vilayat Khan. He has toured abroad extensively.

RAJA BHAIYA POONCHWALÉ Hindustani
(vocalist, also musicologist)
Born in 1882 into a musical family of Gwalior, Raja Bhaiya Poonchwalé is remembered as a fine singer and generous teacher. He learnt from many teachers, the best known being Shankar Rao Pandit.

Raja Bhaiya Poonchwalé assisted V.N. Bhatkhande in his researches and was himself a gifted composer. His pupils include G.N. Natu, V.J. Joshi, M.V. Kalvint and his own son Balasaheb Poonchwalé.

RAJA CHHATRAPATI SINGH Hindustani (*pakhavaj*)
Raja Chhatrapati Singh was born in 1919 and trained with Swami Ram Das. He belongs to the Kudau Singh *gharana* and also plays the *tabla*. Raja Chhatrapati Singh toured Europe with the Dagar Brothers in 1964. He has published a book titled *Mridang Martand*.

RAJESWARI DATTA Hindustani (vocalist)
Rajeswari Datta, who specialized in *Rabindra-sangeet*, was trained at Santiniketan and later studied for many years under the

guidance of Yamini Ganguli. She taught Indian music at London University where she also conducted research.

RAM NARAYAN Hindustani (*sarangi*)
Born in 1927, Ram Narayan comes from a family of musicians. He studied with Mehboob Khan, Mahadeo Prasad and Abdul Wahid Kahn. Ram Narayan has toured the world several times and has made many recordings. In 1968 he taught at Wesleyan University and Mills College, Oakland, in the United States.

RAVI SHANKAR Hindustani (*sitar*, also composer)
Born at Varanasi in 1920, Ravi Shankar comes from a family of cultured Bengali Brahmins. At the age of ten he joined his elder brother, the dancer Uday Shankar, in Paris. He learnt to dance and to play a variety of instruments, and in 1938 he became a pupil of Allauddin Khan with whom he lived for seven years.

Ravi Shankar has composed the music for numerous films and ballets — from Ray's *Apu* trilogy to Davis' *Viola*. His disc recordings sell throughout the world and his book *My Music, My Life* was a bestseller. He founded and directed *Vadya Vrinda*, the national orchestra, and has performed and lectured in most countries of the world. His *Sitar Concerto* was perfomed by the L.S.O. with André Previn as conductor and Ravi Shankar himself playing the *sitar*.

Honoured by many universities, cultural organizations and international bodies, Ravi Shankar has been awarded the Padma Vibhushan. He and his wife Sukanya now live in California.

REHMAT ALI KHAN Hindustani (*sarod*)
Rehmat Ali Khan was born in 1947, the son of Hafiz Ali Khan. He studied with his father and teaches at the Bharatiya Kala Kendra. He has toured the former U.S.S.R. and Europe.

ROSHANARA BEGUM Pakistani (vocalist)
Born in Calcutta in 1924, Roshanara Begum is an outstanding pupil of Abdul Karim Khan. She has made disc recordings and often sings for Radio Pakistan. Roshanara Begum has been honoured by the government of Pakistan.

s.n. ratanjankar Hindustani
(vocalist, also composer and musicologist)
Dr. Ratanjankar was first taught by Pandits Krishnambhatt and
Anant Manohar Joshi. He then became V.N. Bhatkhande's
pupil and later learnt from Faiyaz Khan. A prolific composer,
many of his works were published in *Geet-manjari*. He headed
the Bhatkhande Music College at Lucknow and was elected
Fellow of the Sangeet Natak Akademi in 1963. He made several
disc recordings.

salamat ali khan Pakistani (vocalist)
Born in 1935, in Hoshiarpur district now in the Indian Punjab,
this *khayal* singer belongs to the Sham Chaurasi *gharana*. He
trained under his father Vilayat Ali Khan. Salamat Ali Khan
and his late elder brother Nazakat Ali Khan earned a vast
reputation. Now Salamat Ali Khan is accompanied by his sons
Sharafat, Latafat and Shafqat.

samta prasad misra Hindustani (*tabla*)
Born in 1920, Samta Prasad Misra — who is also known as
Gudia Maharaj — belongs to the Poorab *gharana*. He was
trained by his father Bacha Maharaj and first made his name at
the Allahabad Music Conference in 1942. Since then he has
been a leading *tabla* artist. He has toured abroad extensively
and has many able pupils, among them his sons Kumar and
Kailash.

saraswati bai Karnatic (vocalist)
Saraswati Bai learnt from T. Krishnacharya. Later she studied
Hindustani music with Yakub Ali Khan. She has toured abroad
and has made many recordings. In 1964 Saraswati Bai was
elected Fellow of the Sangeet Natak Akademi.

sebastian k. joseph Karnatic (vocalist also *mridangam*)
Sebastian K. Joseph trained with I.N. Govindan, Kutty Panicker
and K.V. Iyer. He has made many disc recordings.

semmangudi r. srinivasa iyer Karnatic (vocalist)
Born in 1908, Srinivasa Iyer studied under many teachers and
was director of the Central College of Karnatic Music in

Madras. He has published work on Jayadeva and Swati Tirunal. In 1953 he received a Sangeet Natak Akademi award.

SHAKOOR KHAN Hindustani (*sarangi*, also vocalist)
Shakoor Khan, born in 1917, studied with Mehboob Khan and Abdul Wahid Khan. He has toured abroad and has been honoured by the Sangeet Natak Akademi. He was an All India Radio staff artist.

SHARAN RANI Hindustani (*sarod*)
Born in 1929, Sharan Rani is master of an instrument that is always associated with men. Her early training was with Allauddin Khan and later she learnt from his son Ali Akbar Khan. She has made several recordings and has toured many countries. In 1968 she was awarded the Padma Shri.

SHARIF KHAN POONCHWALÉ Pakistani (*sitar*)
Sharif Khan Poonchwalé first learnt from his father Rahim Baksh and then from Inayat Khan. He is a well known *sitar* player and the ruler of Nepal was once his patron. He now lives in Lahore and is a frequent broadcaster.

SHASHANK SUBRAMANIAM Karnatic (flute)
This teen-aged musician displayed an understanding of music from a very early age. Apart from vocal training, under R.K. Srikantan and Palghat K.V. Narayanaswamy, he was also taught the violin. However, he is now making a name for himself as a gifted flute player.

SHIV KUMAR SHARMA Hindustani (*santoor*)
Born in 1938, Shiv Kumar Sharma is a leading exponent of the *santoor* which is now accepted as a concert instrument. He studied with Uma Datt Sharma and has frequently toured in the West.

SIDDESHWARI DEVI Hindustani (vocalist)
Siddeshwari Devi, the daughter of Shamu Misra, was born in Varanasi in 1908. She studied with Siyaji Maharaj, Badé Ramdas and Inayat Khan and is particularly well regarded for her *thumri* and *dadra* singing. She is a Padma Shri and in 1966

was given a Sangeet Natak Akademi award. Siddeshwari Devi teaches at the Bharatiya Kala Kendra and has toured many countries. Her daughter Savita Devi, whom she taught, is also an accomplished singer.

SINGH BANDHU Hindustani (vocalists)
Tejpal Singh and Surinder Singh, born in 1935 and 1938 respectively, are known as Singh Bandhu (Singh Brothers). They first studied with G.S. Sardar, their elder brother, and later with Amir Khan. Their *khayal* singing brings together elements from the Patiala, Kirana and Indore schools. Tejpal and Surinder Singh are well known in India and their recordings are widely appreciated.

SUBBULAKSHMI Karnatic (vocalist)
Subbulakshmi's mother was the celebrated *veena* player Shanmuga Vadivu. Subbulakshmi, born in Madurai in 1916, learnt vocal and instrumental music from her mother, and at seventeen gave her first solo recital. Her singing in the Hindi film *Mira* and the Tamil film *Shakuntala* made her name known in both north and south India. She has since been known as *Kokila*, nightingale.

Subbulakshmi has sung at music festivals all over the world and has made numerous recordings. In 1966 she performed at the opening of the general assembly of the United Nations. She has been honoured by the Sangeet Natak Akademi and in 1954 was made a Padma Bhushan.

SHUSHEELA MISRA Hindustani (vocalist)
A music producer with All India Radio, Susheela Misra toured the United Kingdom in 1964. She sings in the *khayal* style and was trained by G.N. Natu and S.N. Ratanjankar. In 1955 she published *Music Profiles*.

SWAMI PRAJNANANANDA Hindustani
(vocalist, also musicologist)
Born in 1907, Swami Prajnanananda is a *sanyasi* and has mastered *khayal* and *dhrupad*. His teachers were N.B. Dutta, G. Banerjee and H. Mukherjee. He has studied the philosophy of music for many years and has published *Rag-o-Rup* and *The*

Historical Development of Indian Music. In 1963, Swami Prajnanananda was elected Fellow of the Sangeet Natak Akademi.

T.K. JAYARAMA IYER Karnatic (violin)
T.K. Jayarama Iyer has had a long and distinguished career in music. He studied with his father G.K. Iyer and has been honoured by the Madras Music Academy and the Sangeet Natak Akademi. He was conductor and composer with *Vadya Vrinda* and then became music adviser to All India Radio.

T.L. VENKATARAMA IYER Karnatic
(vocalist, also musicologist)
Poet, playwright, and judge of the supreme court of India, T.L. Venkatarama Iyer learnt music from Muthaiah Bhagavatar and Ambi Dikshitar. He has made many recordings and was elected Fellow of the Sangeet Natak Akademi in 1964.

THAKUR JAIDEV SINGH Hindustani
(vocalist, also musicologist)
Author and Fellow or the Sangeet Natak Akademi, Thakur Jaidev Singh trained with S. Harihirlekar and Nanku Bhaiya Telang. He was chief producer with All India Radio and headed the Indian delegation to the 1962 International Music Conference in Tokyo.

TIRUVIZHIMIZHALAI SUBRAMANIA PILLAI
Karnatic (*nadaswaram*)
T. Subramania Pillai and his younger brother N. Sundaram Pillai, the Tiruvizhimizhalai Brothers, are well known in south India. They have made many disc recordings. The elder brother received a Sangeet Natak Akademi award in 1962.

U. SRINIVAS Karnatic (mandolin)
A child prodigy who took South India by storm, 'Mandolin' Srinivas is now well known throughout India and abroad. He has performed with many Western musicians in international music festivals.

v.d. PALUSKAR Hindustani (vocalist)
Pandit Vishnu Digambar Paluskar learnt music from an early age from Balkrishna Bua. Paluskar's powerful voice became famous all over pre-partition India. He founded music colleges — the first at Lahore in 1901 — and used music as an instrument of national reawakening. During his lifetime Paluskar made a few recordings and these are now highly prized.

v.v. SADAGOPAN Karnatic (vocalist, also musicologist)
V.V. Sadagopan, known as Seshadasan Nandan, was professor of Karnatic music at Delhi University. He has made many recordings, has toured abroad, and is the editor of *Indian Music Journal*.

VENKATARAMAN RAGHAVAN Karnatic (musicologist)
Professor of Sanskrit at Madras University and editor of the journal of the Madras Music Academy, V. Raghavan has published a large body of work. He has travelled abroad extensively. He is a Padma Bhushan and was made Fellow of the Sangeet Natak Akademi in 1964.

VILAYAT KHAN Hindustani (*sitar*)
Vilayat Khan, born in 1924, comes from a family of many generations of master musicians. His early training was with his father Inayat Khan and he then studied vocal music with his mother. He therefore developed his own style of *gayaki* playing in which the *sitar* emulates the human voice. To achieve this Vilayat Khan modified his instrument, adjusted his technique and also changed the tuning. He is himself a fine singer.

A musician who can evoke the most delicate lyricism, Vilayat Khan has made many recordings. He has toured abroad several times and in 1964 appeared at the Edinburgh Festival.

VINAY BHARAT-RAM Hindustani (vocalist)
After studying with Ravi Shankar, Ali Akbar Khan and Annapurna Shankar, Vinay Bharat-Ram became an established singer in north India. He has toured the West many times. A Delhi industrialist, Vinay Bharat-Ram is now a leading art patron.

VINAYAK NARAYAN PATWARDHAN Hindustani
(vocalist, also musicologist)
Elected Fellow of the Sangeet Natak Akademi in 1965, V.N.
Patwardhan was principal of the Vishnu Digambar Sangeet
Mahavidyalaya, Poona. He toured Europe in 1964 and has
made disc recordings. His chief books are *Raga Vijnan* and *Bala
Sangeet.* A *khayal* singer of the Gwalior *gharana*, he studied
under Keshavrao Patwardhan and V.D. Paluskar.
V.N. Patwardhan has experience of stage acting and is also a
composer.

VISHNU GOVIND JOG Hindustani (violin)
Professor V.G. Jog is a leading violinist in the field of
Hindustani music. Born in 1922, he studied with V. Shastry,
S.G. Athavale, G. Purohit and S.N. Ratanjankar. He joined All
India Radio in 1953. His publication is titled *Bela Siksha.*
Prof. Jog has toured abroad several times.

VISHNUDAS SHIRALI Hindustani (vocalist, also *sitar*)
Born in 1907, Vishnudas Shirali studied with V.D. Paluskar and
Allauddin Khan. He sings *khayal* of the Gwalior *gharana* and
plays the *sitar* in the style of the Seniya *gharana.* He was
composer and director of Uday Shankar's ballet company and
later joined the films division of the government. He has
published *Hindu Music and Rhythm.*

ZAKIR HUSSEIN and FAZAL QURESHI Hindustani (*tabla*)
The two sons of Alla Rakha are numbered among the most
innovative percussionists of the Indian subcontinent. Zakir
Hussein has earned an international reputation as *tabla* wizard,
cultural ambassador and actor. In 1988 he was honoured with
the Padma Shri and in 1991 won a Sangeet Natak Akademi
award. Fazal Qureshi, the younger brother, is known for his
versatility and energy.

ZIA MOHIUDDIN KHAN DAGAR Hindustani (*been*)
The sole *been* playing member of the Dagar family, Zia
Mohiuddin Khan Dagar is based in Bombay. He has taught in
the United States and has done much to make the *been* more
acceptable to Indian audiences.

GLOSSARY

abhoga: conclusion, also called *samapti*.

ahata nada: "struck sound" which is audible to humans.

alamkara: musical ornamentation.

alap: the beginning; the slow rhythm-free start to a full exposition of a *raga*.

alvars: composers of hymns in south India.

amsa: keynote; now called *vadi*.

anahata nada: "unstruck sound", inaudible to most humans.

andolita: musical swing.

anga: limb. A group of beats, or bar, in a time measure.

antara: musical development in the upper octave, known as *anupallavi* in south India.

anudrut: the time value of a *matra*; between $6/7$ and $3/4$ of a second.

anuvadi: the notes of a *raga* other than the dominant and subdominant.

apsara: celestial nymph.

aroha: ascending note pattern.

ati-drut: very fast tempo.

ati-mandra: very low register.

ati-tar: very high register.

ati-vilambit: very slow tempo; also called *dhima*.

avroha: descending note pattern.

bais: female singers and dancers in north India.

bani: a Hindi word from the Sanskrit which means "language", "precept" or "doctrine". It is also another name for Saraswati, specifically as the goddess of speech. In music, *bani* means "type" or "precept". It is used in connection with the four types of *dhrupad* still in existence. See *dhrupad*.

beej mantra: sacred "seed" words or verse given by a holy man to a disciple.

beenkars: specialists of the *been*, the *veena* of north India. The 16th century saint-musician Tansen had only one daughter and her descendants are known as *beenkars*.

bhagti: a movement which stressed the brotherhood of man.

Its followers employed music and poetry to spread their gospel.

bhajan: religious song; hymn.

Bharata Natyam: literally meaning "Dance of India". See *Dasi Attam*.

bhava: mood, feelings; also the delineation of them.

bheda-bheda: the doctrine which identifies the individual with the Supreme Bring.

boles: recited syllables which assist drummers to master the *tales*, time measures.

cante flamenco: wild and passionate type of song adapted from the *cante hondo* mainly by the gipsies. There are many sub-types of this *genre*.

cante hondo: plaintive type of Andalusian song using intervals smaller than a semitone.

cheeza: song composed for singers of the *Khayal* style.

choot taan: a *taan*, musical figure, that has upward and downward movements at great speed.

dadra: light classical song; also a *tala* of six beats.

darshan: divine visitation; the appearance of an exalted person before lesser mortals.

Dasi Attam: the classical dance of south India; the dance of the *devadasis*, the female temple dancers. This style is now called *Bharata Natyam*.

dastgah: Persian mode.

desi: concerning the countryside; *desa-bhasa* would mean vernaculars, regional dialects, or languages of the countryside.

Desi Sangeet: secular or profane music.

devadasis: temple courtesans who were trained singers and dancers. There were, in south India, many classes of *devadasis*. The *rajadasis* and *alangais*, for example, were educated and highly sophisticated.

dhamar: a type of *tala*. *Dhamars* are also songs in the dialect known as *Braj Bhasa* and tell of the god Krishna during the spring festival of Holi.

dhrupad: the original name of this type of verse, sung in an austere style, was *dhruvapada*. *Dhrupads* were first written in Sanskrit, the classical language of ancient India. Nowadays most songs of this type are in *Braj Bhasa*. The four *banis*, types, of *dhrupad* are named after the places where they first originated. They are: Gaurhar *bani*, Nauhar *bani*, Khandar *bani*, and Dagar *bani*.

dhrupadiyas: singers who follow the *dhrupad* style.

doab: the land lying between two rivers.

drut: the time value of two *matras*.

drut laya: fast tempo.

fakir: Muslim holy man.

gamak: grace note.

gamak taan: a *taan*, musical figure, which repeats notes in virtuoso displays of technique.

ganda-bandhi: ritual of initiation when a master accepts a pupil. The master (*guru* or *ustad*) ties a symbolic thread to the wrist of the pupil (*sishya* or *shahgird*). This makes the pupil the master's "son" for life. The pupil is dressed in white and presents his master with expensive gifts. Some prayers are recited and the master gives the pupil boiled grams and *gur*, jaggery, to eat. The former is to ensure that the pupil gets the strength to create powerful rhythms and the latter ensures that his notes will be pure and sweet. The pupil then reciprocates with an act of devotion which signifies that both strength and sweetness flow from the master. After this the master instructs the pupil in his first formal lesson.

This ceremony starts the *guru-sishya-parampara*, the unbroken tradition that is passed on from master to pupil.

gath: usually the fourth, and final, section of an instrumental performance. *Gaths* are structured compositions, although allowing for improvisation. They end, as it were, in a tornado of rhythm.

gharana: from *ghar*, home. In musical terms it means school or family. Various *gharanas* of music and dance were established by famous artists and teachers. Every *gharana* has, to this day, its distinctive styles and conventions.

ghazals: poems in the Urdu language set to music.

gopees: maidens.

graha: clef.

grama: base. Originally there were three basic or parent
scales: *Sadja-grama, Madhyama-grama,* and *Gandhara-
grama.* Only the first is now in use in a modified form.

guru: spiritual mentor, teacher. In music a *guru* is the time
value of eight *matras.*

guru-sishya-parampara: the sacred relationship between
master and pupil by which knowledge, *gyan,* is transmitted
to the next generation.

hasta: hand gesture in Kathak, the classical dance of north
India. In the south Indian dance styles hand gestures are
called *mudras.*

Hindustani music: the classical music of north India. The
music of Pakistan, Bangladesh and Afghanistan is essentially the same as that of north India.

Holi: spring festival associated with the god Krishna. People
playfully spray coloured water on each other during the
festivities.

ishta-deva: guardian deity.

jabra taan: a *taan,* musical figure, that creates a trembling
effect.

jati: now meaning class or type. *Ragas* today belong to three
classes or *jatis. Jatis* are also complex rhythmic patterns
used in the *Bharata Natyam* dance style of south India. In
ancient times *jatis* were sequences of notes. Bharata used
the term in the sense of a melody archetype.

jātigān: an old musical form which depended on *jatis,*
sequences of notes. *Jātigān* was the precursor of the *raga*
system.

javaabi-sangat: the section in which the percussion instrument
very closely follows and imitates the main instrument.

jhala: the third section of a *raga,* after the *jorh,* played in a
fast tempo.

ji: appended to names out of respect. Hence "Guru-ji" or
"Pandit-ji".

jorh: the second section of a *raga,* after the *alap.* In the *jorh*
some elements of rhythm are introduced.

kakapada: the time value of sixteen *matras*.
kalā: art. In music it is a quarter of a *matra*.
kampita: shake.
Karnatic music: the classical music of south India.
Kathak: the classical dance style of north India.
Kathakali: the classical dance-drama of Kerala in south-west India.
keertan: sung prayer.
khali: empty. The *khalis* are the unstressed beats in a *tala*.
khayal: an imaginative style of north Indian singing.
khayaliyas: singers who follow the *khayal* style.
komal: flat note.
kritis: religious songs in south India. The *kritis* of Thyagaraja are particularly famous.
kumbhasthūn: a percussion instrument made of an earthern pot with leather stretched over its mouth. This instrument was developed and used by the *vaitālikas*, Buddhist religious singers.
kut taan: a *taan*, musical figure, that moves in a zig-zag manner.

lagan: attachment to, or longing for, something.
laghu: the time value of four *matras*.
larant: the rhythmic competition between the percussion and the stringed instrument.
lasya: feminine. Applied to the dance of Parvati, Shiva's divine consort.
laya: tempo.
lingam: penis. The god Shiva's *lingam* symbolized fertility and procreation and was thus an object of veneration.

madhya: middle or medium.
madhya drut: medium fast tempo.
madhya laya: medium tempo.
madhya sthan: middle register.
madhya vilambit: medium slow tempo.
madhura nada: sound pleasing to the ear.
mandra: low register corresponding to the bass.
maqam: Arabic mode.
Mārga Sangeet: sacred music.

matra: a beat.

meend: slide.

melakarta: basic parent scale of south Indian classical music.
There are 72 *melakartas*, classified by Venkatamakhi in the
17th century.

mirh: slur.

moksha: liberation of the soul.

muni: sage.

murchana: mode.

nada: sound. The word has peculiar philosophical connotations. *Nada* is cosmic energy; it is the First Cause. Chanted
sounds such as *"Aum"* (written thus: ॐ) symbolize the
creative power of *nada*.

nattuvanars: south Indian musicians and dance teachers who
were usually the sons of *devadasis*.

nayakas: heroes, lovers, worthies. Beautiful women, loved by
nayakas, are called *nayikas*.

nimesa: 1/32 of a *matra*. In practice *nimesas* are grouped in
fours, so that each group is 1/8 of a *matra*.

nritta: pure dance; as opposed to *nritya*, dance which tells a
story or conveys an emotion.

nritya: see *nritta* above.

nyasa. cadence.

odava: *raga* which uses five notes.

padam: danced love lyric in *Bharata Natyam*.

pakad: catch phrase by which a *raga* is easily identified.

pandit: learned person; term of respect for Brahmins, the
highest Hindu caste.

parans: variations of *thekas*. In the *Kathak* dance style a *paran*
is a fast piece set to the syllabic beats of the *pakhavaj*.

pluta: the time value of twelve *matras*.

puranas: stories concerning the gods.

purvanga: lower tetrachord.

qawals: singers of *qawwalis*.

qawwali: form of Muslim religious singing in which many
voices are used.

rababiyas: specialists of the *rabab*, a stringed instrument invented by Tansen. The descendants of Tansen's four sons are called *rababiyas*.

Rabindra-sangeet: the lyrical style of music propagated by Rabindranath Tagore.

raga: a combination of notes, aesthetically pleasing, and capable of "colouring the hearts of men". Technically, a scale, a melody archetype.

ragini: a female *raga*; a *raga's* "wife". The *ragini* was supposed to represent the female aspect of a *raga*. The term is no longer in use.

ranj: to colour with emotion.

rasa: emotional state, sentiment. There are now nine recognized *rasas* known as *Nava-rasas*.

riyaz: practice.

sādava: *ragas* which use six notes.

sadhana: dedication. Also spiritual preparation and musical practice.

sadhu: Hindu holy man.

salamu: from *salaam*, Muslim salutation. *Salamus*, salutations, are used in the *Bharata Natyam* dance. Nowadays the term *charnam*, which is also the last part of a poem, is used in place of *salamu*.

samadhi: shrine.

sāmagān: ancient form of vocal music which was sung in three tonal accents and not to the seven musical notes.

sampūrna: complete. *Sampūrna ragas* use all the seven notes.

samvadi: subdominant note of a *raga*.

sanchari: mixed; unconventional ascents and descents in the motions of a *raga*.

sandhiprakash: twilight. The *sandhiprakash ragas* are sung or played during dusk and dawn.

sangat: accompaniment; usually of the percussion with the main instrument.

sangathis: musical phrases in Karnatic music.

sangeet: a word with wide meaning for it includes vocal and instrumental music, theatre, and dance.

sanyasi: an ascetic, a mendicant.

saptak: the seven notes (SA, RE, GA, MA, PA, DHA, NI) of

the Indian 'octave'.

sargam: sol-fa passages.

savaal-javaab: question-answer session between the main instrument and the percussion. Many musicians call this *javaab-savaal* (answer-question) which is somewhat confusing.

shabdam: danced song in *Bharata Natyam*.

shanta: peace, tranquillity, serenity.

shastras: books held sacred by the Hindus.

sishya: disciple; the other word for disciple is *shahgird*.

sloka: Sanskrit verse.

sollukuttus: dance syllables of *Bharata Natyam*.

sruti: "to hear" in Sanskrit. A microtone. There are 22 *srutis* generally recognized in Indian music.

sthans: positions. In music it means registers.

sthayi: repetition or unchanging. Known as the *pallavi* in south India; the *sthayi* establishes the theme, usually in the lower octave.

suddha: pure, natural.

sufism: a Muslim philosophy which encouraged mysticism; like the *bhagti* movement of Hinduism it relied heavily on music and poetry.

sum: the most important beat in a *tala*.

swara: note. A *suddha swara* is the equivalent of a natural note.

swara varna: ascending or descending runs of notes.

taan: musical figure: a succession of notes. Narada claimed that there were 490 million *taans!*

tala: time measure. Every *tala* has a set number of beats divided up into bars.

tala vadya kacheri: south Indian ensemble for percussion instruments.

tali: clap. The *talis* are the stressed beats of a *tala*. A *tali* is also a south Indian wedding necklace.

tanas: Bharata used this term to describe those *murchanas* which had overlapping notes.

tandav: the masculine element. Applied to the virile dance of the god Shiva.

tappas: songs of the camel drivers of the Punjab which were

refined and introduced into the classical repertoire by
Miyań Shori. The *tappa* style is well known for its ornamen-
tations.

tar: treble.

tarana: type of singing in fast tempo which uses syllables.
When pieced together these syllables form Persian words
that have mystic symbolism.

tavaifs: courtesans of north India well known for their singing
and dancing.

thaat: a group of *ragas*. There are ten accepted *thaats* in north
India.

theka: basic percussion phrase which identifies a *tala*.

Thumri Andaaz: the special method of interpreting a *thumri*
in the Kathak dance. The dancer sits down and sings and
mimes a romantic lyric.

thumris: romantic lyrics.

tillana: brilliant pure dance section in the *Bharata Natyam*
style.

tirmana: a quick succession of dance units in *Bharata Natyam*.

tivra: sharp note.

tribhanga: dance pose with three bends in the body.

trimurti: the Hindu trinity or triad of gods: Brahma, Vishnu,
and Shiva.

truti: half a *matra*.

ustad: master; the title used by Muslim musicians of merit.

uttranga: upper tetrachord.

vadi: dominant note of a *raga*.

vaitālikas: early Buddhist religious singers.

varna: colour; also caste.

Vedas: Hindu scriptures.

vibhag: another word for *anga*.

vikrit: altered, modified.

vilambit laya: slow tempo.

vistar: elaboration or improvisation; extended exposition.

vivadi: dissonant notes which destroy the mood or colour of a
raga. Occasionally used by expert musicians in order to
create a special effect.

Wayang Kulit: the art of shadow puppetry very popular in Malaysia. The puppets are made of coloured leather and are flat. They are manipulated by a puppeteer — the *dalang* — and their shadows are projected on to a screen. The stories of the puppet dramas are taken from the Indian epics.

yogi: a mystic, seer.

zamindars: feudal landlords. The princes (maharajas, rajas, and nawabs) and the *zamindars* were the chief patrons of music and dance before India's independence.

LIST OF USEFUL ADDRESSES

Several Indian universities have music and dance departments. There are also many institutes and academies that specialize in particular music and dance styles. Enquiries may be addressed to the following:

The Indian Council for Cultural
    Relations,
Azad Bhavan,
Indraprastha Estate,
New Delhi 110 002,
India.

Department of Culture,
Ministry of Human Resource Development,
Shastri Bhavan,
New Delhi 110 001,
India.

Sangeet Natak Akademi,
Rabindra Bhavan,
Ferozeshah Road,
New Delhi 110 001,
India.

Darpana Centre for the Performing Arts,
Ahmedabad,
Gujarat State,
India.

Kadamb Centre for Dance and Music,
Parimal Garden,
C.G. Road,
Ahmedabad 380 006,
Gujarat State,
India.

Bhatkhande Sangeet Vidyapith,
Lucknow,
Uttar Pradesh,
India.

The Madras Music Academy,
Madras,
Tamil Nadu,
India.

Bharatiya Vidya Bhavan,
KM Munshi Marg,
Chowpatty,
Bombay 400 007,
India.

The Kalakshetra Academy of Music and
    Dance,
Tiruvanmiyur,
Madras 600 041,
Tamil Nadu,
India.

Indira Gandhi Centre for the Performing
    Arts,
Vigyan Bhavan,
New Delhi 110 001,
India.

Bharatiya Vidya Bhavan,
4A Castletown Road,
West Kensington,
London W14 9HQ,
England.

Balasaraswati Center of Music and Dance,
P.O. Box 227,
Prince Station,
New York, NY 10012,
U.S.A.

BIBLIOGRAPHY

This bibliography does not purport to be a comprehensive one on the subject. It is, rather, a selective list of books in English which the reader might find useful.

Classical Indian Dance in Literature and the Arts: Kapila Vatsyayan (Sangeet Natak Akademi, New Delhi, 1968)

Discovery of India: Jawaharlal Nehru (Meridian Books, London, 1946)

Hindu Manners, Customs and Ceremonies: Abbé Dubois (O.U.P. 1906)

Hindu Scriptures: Nicol Macnicol (Dent, London, 1938)

Hindustani Music, An Outline of Its Physics and Aesthetics: G.H. Ranade (Sangli, 1938)

India, A Short Cultural History: H.G. Rawlinson (Cresset Press, London, 1937)

Indian Music — A Vast Ocean of Promise: Peggy Holroyde (Allen & Unwin, London, 1972)

India's Heritage: Humayun Kabir (Meridian Books, London, 1947)

Life and Works of Amir Khusro: M.W. Mirza (Punjab University, 1935)

Melodic Types of Hindustan: N.K. Bose (Jaico Publishing House, Bombay, 1960)

Music and Dance in Indian Art: Philip Rawson (Edinburgh Festival Society, 1963)

Music East and West: Indian Council for Cultural Relations (New Delhi, 1966)

My Music, My Life: Ravi Shankar (Simon & Schuster, New York, 1968)

Natya Shastra: Bharata, trans. Manomohan Ghosh (Royal Asiatic Society of Bengal, Calcutta, 1950)

The Erotic Sculpture of India: Max-Pol Fouchet, trans. Brian Rhys (Allen & Unwin, London, 1959)

The Music of Hindostan: A. H. Fox Strangways (Clarendon Press, Oxford, 1965 reprint)

The Music of India: Herbert A. Popley (O.U.P. 1921)

The Ragas of North India: Walter Kaufmann (Indiana University Press, 1968)

The Raga-s of Northern Indian Music: Alain Daniélou (Barrie & Cresset, London, 1968)

The Rags of North Indian Music: N.A. Jairazbhoy (Faber, London, 1971)

The Rise of Music in the Ancient World — East and West: Curt Sachs (Dent, London, 1943)

The Sanskrit Drama: A.B. Keith (Clarendon Press, Oxford)

The Story of Indian Music: O. Goswami (Asia Publishing House, Bombay, 1961)

Who's Who of Indian Musicians: (Sangeet Natak Akademi, New Delhi, 1968)

The Dances of India: Reginald & Jamila Massey (Tricolour Books, London, 1989)

All India: Reginald Massey (Apple, London, 1986)

The Life of Music in North India: Daniel M. Neuman (University of Chicago Press, 1990)

Music and Musical Thought in Early India: Lewis Rowell (University of Chicago Press, 1992)

Sitar Music in Calcutta: James Sadler Hamilton (University of Calgary Press, 1989)

Hindustani Music in the Twentieth Century: Wim Van Der Meer (Martinus Nijhoff Publishers, The Hague, 1980)

Filigree in Sound: Gopal Sharman (Vikas, New Delhi, 1970)

The Historical Development of Indian Music: Swami Prajnanananda (Firma K.L. Mukhopadhyay, Calcutta, 1960)

The Wonder that was India: A.L. Basham (Macmillan, New York, 1954)

Music in India: the classical traditions: Bonnie C. Wade (Prentice-Hall, New Jersey, 1979)

DISCOGRAPHY

Listed below are a few records representative of the many types of Indian music. The Import Sales Department of EMI at Hayes, Middlesex, (telephone 573 3888) can be contacted for information regarding other releases.

India I (Vedic chant): BM 30 L2006
    Recorded and annotated by Alain Daniélou.
India III (Dhrupad): BM 30 L2018
    Recorded and annotated by Alain Daniélou.
Karnatic Music: UNESCO Series
    Recorded and annotated by John Levy.
Balachander (veena): HMV ECLP 2270
Shrimati Subbulakshmi (vocal): HMV ECLP 2293
West meets East: ALP/ASD 2294
    Yehudi Menuhin (violin) and Ravi Shankar *(sitar)*
Music from India, Vol I: ALP/ASD 2295
    Vilayat Khan *(sitar)* and Bismillah Khan *(shehnai)*.
Music from India, Vol II: ALP/ASD 2304
    Ravi Shankar *(sitar)* and Ali Akbar Khan *(sarod)*.
Music from India, Vol III: ALP/ASD 2312
    Bismillah Khan *(shehnai)* and V.G. Jog (violin).
Khan Sahib Abdul Karim Khan (vocal): Columbia 33 ECX 3253
Bhimsen Joshi (vocal): HMV EALP 1280
Ustad Faiyaz Khan Sahib (vocal): HMV EALP 1292
Amir Khan (vocal): HMV EALP 1253
Hirabai Barodekar (vocal): HMV ECLP 2275
Anthology of Indian Classical Music: UNESCO Series: DTL 93111-3. Collected by Alain Daniélou.
Musique Populaire de l'Inde du Nord, Musée de l'Homme: MC 20. 110, Collected by Deben Bhattacharya.
Folk Music of India (Orissa): Lyrichord LL ST7183
    Collected by N.A. Jairazbhoy.
Morning and Evening Ragas: HMV ALPC 2
    Ali Akbar Khan *(sarod)* and Chatur Lal *(tabla)*. Introduced by Yehudi Menuhin.

Indian Music: World Pacific WP 1248
Ravi Shankar (*sitar*) and Chatur Lal (*tabla*).
The Ragas of India: Folkways FL 8368
An introduction to *ragas* by B.R. Deodhar.
Alla Rakha (*tabla*): HMV 7EPE 1252
Pannalal Ghosh (flute): HMV EALP 1252
Vilayat Khan (*sitar*): HMV EALP 1266
Bade Ghulam Ali Khan (vocal): HMV EALP 1256
Rahimuddin Khan Dagar (vocal): HMV 7EPE 1206
Nazakat Ali and Salamat Ali (vocal): HMV EALP 1264
Pandit Omkarnath Thakur (vocal): Columbia 33 EC 3751
Roshanara Begum (vocal): HMV 1530
Ali Akbar Khan (sarod)): EMI ECSD 2587
Ustad Ghulam Mustafa Khan (vocal): Polydor 2392 934
Bade Ghulam Ali Khan (vocal): EMI MAOE 5004
Bade Ghulam Ali Khan (vocal): EMI MAOE 5005
Ravi Shankar and André Previn: EMI ASD 2752
Shankar Concerto for *sitar* and orchestra; with the London Symphony Orchestra
Bhimsen Joshi (vocal): EMI S-MOAE 5010
Ghulam Ali (vocal): Music India 2393 951
Roshanara Begum (vocal): EMI CLP 1514
Salamat Ali (vocal): EMI Pakistan LKDA 20057
Habib Ali Khan Beenkar (vichitra veena): EMI Pakistan ALPC 13
Ragas Hameer & Gara: Deutsche Grammophon 2531 216
Ravi Shankar *(sitar)* and Alla Rakha *(tabla).* Note by Ellen Hickmann
Raga Jogeshwari: Deutsche Grammophon 2351 280
Ravi Shankar *(sitar)* and Alla Rakha *(tabla).* Note by Ellen Hickmann
Homage to Mahatma Gandhi and Baba Allauddin: Deutsche Grammophon 2351 356
Ravi Shankar *(sitar)* and Alla Rakha *(tabla).* Note by Reginald Massey

Index

Index 189